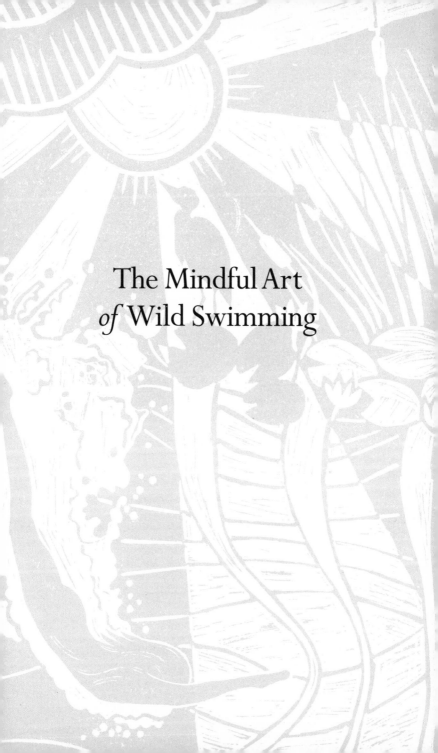

The Mindful Art
of Wild Swimming

The Mindful Art
of Wild Swimming

Reflections for Zen Seekers

Tessa Wardley

Leaping Hare Press

First published in the UK in 2017 by

Leaping Hare Press

An Imprint of The Quarto Group
The Old Brewery, 6 Blundell Street
London N7 9BH, United Kingdom
T (0)20 7700 6700
www.Quarto.com

British Library Cataloguing-in-Publication Data
A catalogue record for this book is available from the British Library

ISBN: 978-1-78240-429-3

This book was conceived, designed and produced by

Leaping Hare Press

Publisher SUSAN KELLY
Creative Director MICHAEL WHITEHEAD
Art Director WAYNE BLADES
Editorial Director TOM KITCH
Commissioning Editor MONICA PERDONI
Senior Project Editor CAROLINE EARLE
Designer GINNY ZEAL
Illustrator TESSA WARDLEY

Printed in China

7 9 10 8 6

Disclaimer

Swimming in an open water environment is undertaken at your own risk and
you should investigate any open water swimming location for local laws and restrictions.
The author and publisher specifically disclaim any responsibility for any liability, loss or risk
(personal, financial or otherwise) that may be claimed or incurred as a consequence – directly
or indirectly – of the use and/or application of any of the contents of this publication.

Contents

Introduction 6

CHAPTER ONE
Taking the Plunge 23

CHAPTER TWO
The Solo Swim 41

CHAPTER THREE
Swimming with Friends 63

CHAPTER FOUR
Swimming Adventures 81

CHAPTER FIVE
Reflections from the Riverbank 103

CHAPTER SIX
Water Wisdom 123

Further Reading & Websites 140
The Mindfulness Series 141
Index 142
Acknowledgements 144

Introduction

When we master the art of swimming,
we discover the liberation that comes with
weightlessness and enter an intensely private world
where a meditative state of mind is easily achieved.
Swimming in wild waters takes this experience to an
even more intense level where self-discovery and
fulfilment reside, producing profound effects on the
mind and spirit. If you are prepared to risk a
certain obsession with water, embark on your
own journey into wild waters. Leap in!

A LOVE OF SWIMMING

◆

All around the world, people love to swim. Young or old, wobbly or trim, firm or infirm – to the water we are all equal. But what draws us back time after time? For me, it is enough to know that I always leave the water feeling happy.

WHEN I WAS THREE YEARS OLD, my mother took me along to our local swimming pool. I went straight to the deep end and jumped off the side. The instructor, Jane, luckily appreciated my enthusiasm but I'm sure raised her eyes to the sky a little as she hooked me out by the back of my swimsuit and set about the task of teaching me to swim. I was lucky to have a mother who wanted me to swim and lucky to have such an inspirational swimming teacher and coach from an early age. I swam with her throughout my school years and when I was a teenager she would embarrass me in front of the swimming club by telling them tales of our first encounter and how she had to rescue me from the deep end. I was undoubtedly a challenging pupil – the memories of my early swimming lessons are all viewed through a column of water, the images shimmering and rippling in my mind's eye as I gaze up at my teacher imparting her words of wisdom. I'm not sure how you teach a child who is constantly underwater but happily she persevered and inspired in me a complete joy of swimming that set me off on my aquatic adventures.

Jane herself is a beautiful swimmer and would often tell us tales of her swimming companions; one friend, in her eighties, apparently had the most wonderful posture and would walk regally beside the pool before starting her daily training. Jane used this example to show us what a wonderful lifetime skill swimming could be and how it would help us physically and keep us fit and healthy right into old age. That first swimming teacher of mine is now herself in her eighties and completely fits the example of the lady she had described to us, tall and fit and regal in her posture; she continues to be an inspiration to many and still out-swims most younger swimmers.

The Perfect Exercise

Swimming really is the most perfect physical exercise. The body, supported by the dense medium of water, gets a cardiovascular workout without the wear and tear of land-based exercise and you develop flexibility and strength as you have to work against the weight of the water. The rhythmic nature of the stroke encourages regular breathing patterns, improving lung efficiency in terms of the volume of air moved in and out at each breath and the oxygen uptake – it's great for asthma suffers. Swimming is a whole-body workout – it works your core, your glutes, hamstrings and shoulders. On top of that, swimming makes you younger – no, really! Research at Indiana University's Counsilman Center for the Science of Swimming has shown that regular swimmers are biologically twenty years younger than their chronological age suggests – swimming can have positive effects on age markers such as blood pressure, cardiovascular performance, the central nervous system, cognitive functioning, muscle mass and blood chemistry.

But swimming is not just good for the body, it is also good for the spirit. Have you ever noticed how positive you feel after a swim and how that feeling lingers for some time? There is a growing body of evidence that points to the mental health benefits of swimming. Just being around water inspires a sense of calm and tranquillity, and immersion in the water just accentuates that further. The activity of swimming encourages social interaction as well as clearing the mind and boosting positivity, all of which promotes feelings of self-worth. Being in the water quite literally buoys you up.

GOING WILD

A century ago, before the era of polluted natural waters and the fully packaged swimming pool experience, virtually all swimming was done outdoors. But now that era is waning, and more people are drawn to reconnecting with the wild – and discovering wild waters.

ALONGSIDE MY FORMAL POOL-SWIMMING LESSONS, I was introduced to wild waters by my parents. I have an old photo that sums up my family holidays. The picture was taken in Scotland – we used to spend our summer holidays camping beside a sea loch on the north-west coast, plagued by midges and heavy rainfall. I am being dangled in crystal-clear waters by my mother, who has a huge smile on her face – I am not yet two years old but I too am smiling and around us my older brothers and sister are lolling and splashing, covering us all with spray. It must have been freezing – I have returned to swim in Scottish waters in recent years, late summer and still achingly cold – but we all look relaxed and happy.

And that is a large element of my childhood – looked at through the lens of my adult life, it is measured in the water-bodies we used to frequent. Coming from Norfolk in eastern England, an island within an island surrounded by water on three sides, our weekends were spent on the broads and the coast. Easters were spent in my aunt's hotel on Exmoor, fishing and playing in the rivers; summers were alongside the sea lochs of Scotland, later the lakes of Sweden, and then moving on to the water-based wilderness of the Lake District and the rivers and coasts of France. It is no surprise, then, that I went on to study marine biology and freshwater ecology, working and travelling globally, and immersing myself in water at every possible opportunity.

New Waters Are Always Flowing
Whether back home in landlocked Surrey or off on my travels, I still love swimming. I love swimming anywhere in the world but once you push away from the wall in a pool they are all

fairly similar – like a McDonald's, a swimming pool swim is much the same in Brisbane, Bangalore, Beijing and Brighton. The memories from the pool merge into one. By comparison, a daily dip in wild waters soon brings truth to that oft-quoted fifth-century philosopher of flux, Heraclitus, who famously said: 'You can never step into the same stream, for new waters are always flowing on to you.'

I have dipped in the gelid waters of the Arctic Circle in Norway, relished a refreshing stretch-out swim in the lakes of the Flinders Ranges of Australia, and been thwarted by my desire to cross lakes in Sweden. I've luxuriated in the warm ebb and flow of a summer Aegean Sea and shivered in the gut-wrenching cold of a winter's Atlantic swim. Every body of water has its own feel and its own memory. Wild water changes by the minute, the day and the season. Exposure to the elements and the surrounding wildlife changes wild swimming into a completely different experience. Every swim is an adventure, forming indelible memories; you will never forget a wild swim. It may not be possible to get out to wild waters every day and I will never stop swimming in pools but I believe that, like garlic foraged from your local woods, water is best when it is wild.

Just being around water inspires
a sense of calm and tranquillity

MINDFULNESS

◆

We all have within our reach an opportunity to really turn up in our lives, to live every moment as if it mattered, this moment right here and now. That opportunity can be taken through the practice of mindfulness, and it can be transformational.

DESPITE EVERYTHING THAT YOU OWN and have access to, do you sometimes feel that something in your life is missing? Do you think that what may be missing is you? It is a sad fact that in our busy lives we rush around in a frenzy trying to respond to all the demands put upon us from phones, emails, social media, bosses, children, pets, parents and spouses – the list goes on. If you have noticed that life may be passing you by, then that is an important observation. The challenge now is to act to resolve the problem and that is where the practice of mindfulness can help.

Like swimming in wild waters, mindfulness is not a new phenomenon. With its roots in Buddhism, mindfulness has been around for two and a half thousand years but, like wild swimming, it is undergoing something of a resurgence in the Western world. This is partly down to scientific research, which has been able to measure the tangible health benefits of mindfulness, prompting a surge of interest. Although its roots are in religion, mindfulness is not a religious activity – it can be practised by anyone of any religious or philosophical persuasion. From the trading floor to the boardroom, mindfulness is being advocated; you can even buy apps that lead you through your mindfulness practice, help you reach your goals and put you in contact with a mindfulness community.

The Aim of Mindfulness

The main thing to understand about mindfulness is that, like most valuable skills, it may not come quickly. It is referred to as a practice because it is a skill that needs to be learned. You can decide you need to be more attentive and aware in your life, which is great, but without training and practice it is hard to achieve; like a muscle that requires exercise and strengthening, mindfulness needs to be worked at, and the more you practise, the more your efforts are rewarded.

The usual practice of mindfulness would see you sitting on a mat, cross-legged, or on a chair, eyes gazing, relaxed, at a point somewhere in front of you. In this position, you carry out your regular sitting meditation – focusing on your breathing and your body. A common misconception about mindfulness is that practitioners are aiming to achieve a kind of blissed-out blank. This could not be further from the truth – the aim of mindfulness is actually to be in a state where we are fully engaged in the present.

It is in moments of extreme stress, when the brain is scrambled and the adrenaline surge is at its highest, that people tend to freeze and the mind goes truly blank. During our mindful practice, we aim to be fully aware of what is going on in our mind while focusing on our breathing and the sensations of our body. Without judgement, we notice these thoughts as they bubble up to the surface. Rather than wrestling with them, we aim to leave these thoughts to one side as we constantly return to our focus. If our practice goes well, we will notice our minds quieten, our thoughts smoothing out like ripples dying out on water.

Negative to Positive

We can be very attached to our thoughts, to the extent where they dominate our sense of self. The majority of our thoughts are dictated by plans, abstractions, fears and anxieties – they often prevent us being attentive to the matter in hand, so that we miss the moment. In the extreme, thoughts can cause negative spirals, whipping up whirlpools of anxiety and depression. If we can learn to put those agitated thoughts to one side to release our smooth-flowing minds, our true selves come to the fore, fully engaged and aware.

Mindfulness can bring back control and free up the reservoirs of our minds, helping us to be more curious and learn more. Being aware in the moment brings spring-like clarity, enabling us to identify which aspects of our lives are unwholesome and wrong, and those that are wholesome and right – we can then take responsibility and make good choices. On the surface, mindfulness may appear to be rather a selfish pursuit but understanding ourselves enables us to understand others better, communicate better, develop better relationships and act with compassion. A positive spiral towards health and happiness.

MINDFULNESS AND WILD SWIMMING

◆

At first glance, wild swimming may not immediately present itself as an obvious activity to align with the practice of mindfulness. However, research is increasingly showing a strong positive link between natural waters and mental health.

THE INCIDENCE OF MENTAL HEALTH ISSUES and social and cultural dysfunctionality is increasing in our developed societies, but research studies have shown the benefits of being outdoors in terms of decreasing anxiety and increasing well-being, and the value of green spaces in inner city areas is finally being recognized. That same research shows that being outside beside water has an even greater beneficial effect. And it doesn't stop there. There is strong evidence to show that immersion in water is beneficial for mind and body and has profound healing effects. Swimmers live longer and are happier than even their walking and running friends. Anyone who has swum in the wild will tell you about the endorphin high that buoys you up, raises the spirits and leaves you feeling eager for more.

The Perfect Partnership

Mindfulness is not an easy skill to master. On some days the tranquil waters of the mind are easily achieved, on others you may feel you are drowning in a maelstrom. You would think that sitting quietly doing mindfulness practice would be the easiest way to perfect your skills but it can actually be hard to stay in the moment while you are inactive. Sometimes it is easier to be engaged in the moment and take notice while performing another task, and wild swimming is the perfect activity to align with mindfulness. Swimming requires careful coordination of the mind, the body and the breath, while mindfulness practice requires you to focus on three things: your mind, your body and your breath. Practising the arts of wild swimming and mindfulness together encourages the development of both skills.

When I talk to other swimmers about their experiences, they usually start by describing how they feel when first getting into the water. This is always a key moment for wild swimmers. The sensations of the body are brought into sharp focus, instantly bringing the swimmer into the here and now.

◆

Science is revealing that there is an
additional simple, watery means to mindfulness.

FROM 'BLUE MIND'
WALLACE J. NICHOLS, AMERICAN MARINE BIOLOGIST

◆

Finding the Flow

In the first few minutes of a swim, it can be hard not to focus on problems and issues that are at the forefront of your daily life, but after a while these slip away and you find yourself focusing more and more on your breathing and finding the rhythm of the stroke. Quite regularly, swimmers reach a point where they feel at peace with their emotions; everything is in perfect balance physically and they are just going with the flow. If you have ever practised a creative art or a sport, you will have experienced such moments of flow or being 'in the zone'. This is also a perfect state of mindfulness – we have let go of our thoughts and our conscious self and have only total engagement with the matter in hand. When people experience these perfect moments of mindfulness, they often describe the moment as when they were 'fully immersed' in their activity, things were 'going swimmingly', and they were 'in the flow'. It is no coincidence that these watery metaphors are employed to describe such moments.

The feelings of happiness and well-being that being in the flow engenders can lead to genuine elation and feed the addiction of wild swimming. It also drives slightly evangelical traits in wild swimmers. You have been warned.

Once the water has their full attention and they start swimming, most swimmers talk about how they focus on the rhythm of their strokes and marry them to their breathing. Many people describe how they feel so alive, calm and focused; feeling the water and letting the strokes flow. An almost identical vocabulary is used by the practitioners of mindfulness and meditation. It appears that wild swimming is facilitating that state of mindfulness.

JOURNEY INTO THE WILD

Endeavouring to find your Zen while perfecting the mindful art of wild swimming is a journey of discovery. We may be familiar with both wild swimming and mindfulness, but by considering the two together we open up the possibility of seeing the world from an entirely new perspective.

FROM OUR FIRST PLUNGE INTO WILD WATERS, we are on that journey. Our early strokes are tentative, with our heads held tensely out of the cold water and our brains frantically working overtime, imagining the grotesqueness of the wild world around our frantically kicking legs – until one day we begin to master the art and can launch out leisurely and relaxed, floating on our backs, enjoying the sky and the wind on our faces, revelling in the rippling of the natural waters as they massage our back and play in our ears.

The only true voyage of
discovery … would be not to visit strange
lands but to possess other eyes.

FROM 'REMEMBRANCE OF THINGS PAST'
MARCEL PROUST 1871–1922, FRENCH NOVELIST

Embarking on any new phase of learning follows a well-recognized pattern of consciousness and competence. As we set out, we are blissfully unaware of our lack of knowledge – we are unconsciously incompetent. Gradually, the realization dawns that the skills we aspire to are not so easily attained and we see quite how far we still have to travel – we are now consciously incompetent. As time goes by, we practise and experience more; we are developing the skills but we have to concentrate and work quite hard to stay on track – we can now be considered consciously competent. Finally, after an extended period of practice and consolidation we suddenly realize that we have mastered the skill, which we are carrying out without even being aware that we are doing it – we are now unconsciously competent.

Discovering Cycles

A water droplet, too, has its own journey; from the freshest spring bubbling to the surface on a hillside the young river grows, playfully gambolling off on its course, growing rapidly to an industrious, transporting, ground-breaking torrent. It flows fast on its steady course, cutting down into the lowlands, forging its route; and then slowly, towards the end of its travels, it meanders as if trying to put off the inevitable – or maybe it has forgotten its urgency to reach the goal and is enjoying the journey. Eventually, the water reaches the sea to play in the freedom of the oceans, circulating around the Earth in fast-flowing currents, languishing in landlocked seas, pushed and pulled by the lunar cycles, only to evaporate into the skies and start the cycle again.

The natural world is driven by daily and seasonal cycles, created by our planet spinning on its axis as it orbits the sun. The year journeys on through the seasons – bursting into life in spring, blooming into the riot of summer, maturing into autumn and hunkering down and consolidating in winter, only to be reborn again. Within these physical cycles, animals and plants entwine their own patterns of living, season by season, year on year; birth, life and death.

Throughout this book, we will be immersing ourselves in learning the mindful art of wild swimming, combining the physical and spiritual cycles of human life with the cycles we encounter as we join the journey of rivers and the ebb and flow of the seas; experiencing the changing seasons and the changing nature of wild waters throughout the world as we develop our swimming needs mindfully.

Are you ready for a wild adventure?

CHAPTER ONE

TAKING THE PLUNGE

Swimming in the wild is something man has done throughout his story. We instinctively know that water is calming, inspiring and brings us peace — so take the plunge and immerse yourself in the health-giving depths. Relish the feelings of fear and excitement; acknowledge them but don't be controlled by them. As you relax into the flow, your breathing becomes one with your movements, ebbing and flowing with the rhythm of the waves. Your mind calms, achieving a stillness and clarity to match that of a mountain pool.

REBIRTH

◆

As you take those first tentative strokes into wild swimming, you are
embarking on a new cycle in your life. From the Maya to the Ancient
Egyptians, in Hinduism, Christianity and Islam, water is revered as
a symbol of cleansing, birth and renewal. Think of this as your own
personal journey of rebirth.

WHEN I WAS YOUNGER, swimming was a part of my life
that I rarely reflected on; I just swam whenever and
wherever – lake, sea, river, open-air pool – and had many
hours of fun and hilarity. Wild swimming was not a 'thing' in
those days. It's only in recent years that swimming has been
categorized into 'wild' or tame. Alongside wild swimming's
categorization, I also became aware of mindfulness as a concept.
Not only was I aware of swimming in natural waters being a
recognized (if slightly subversive) activity but I was taking part
in such a way that I was more thoughtful of my actions.

This mindfulness was quite transformative in the way it
allowed me to approach my experiences in the outdoors.
It happened that my first swims as a labelled 'wild swimmer'
were in the newborn mountain streams of the Pyrenees. The
power of water is fully evident in these mountain environments; our frailty in the face of nature is all too apparent in
the rock formations carved out of the mountains, themselves
thrown up by the movements of the Earth's crust. The new-

Everything was new, fresh, alive and
wonderful... There was nothing holding
me back. There were no walls, no black lines ...
I was surrounded by the wide-open
sea and the infinite sky...

FROM 'SWIMMING TO ANTARCTICA'
LYNNE COX, AMERICAN OPEN-WATER SWIMMER

---

born river has done its work over the years and it makes me
feel very small and insignificant, humble in the face of nature's
strength. This may be why I have a love of the effervescent,
crystal-clear waters churning in a young boulder-strewn
river, river cliffs delineating the limpid green pools where
every underwater feature is visible and fish dart to the side as
you swim by. Nothing could be, or make you feel, more alive.

The Spirit of Adventure

The swims are brief as we make our way along the channel;
no more than five or ten strokes are needed to cross most
pools and then we clamber, slide or jump over smoothed rock
stands, chutes and cliffs. The spirit of adventure feels strong as
we fall into the rhythm of the river – the way it moves through
the landscape, the pattern of turns and barriers and pools
dictated by the geology. Often we find ourselves deep below
the surface of the surrounding land in gorges and gullies cut

Pre-swim Planning

How are you going to embark on your first strokes as a mindful wild swimmer? Will you match your experiences with a newly born upland river or mountain tarn, or a middle-aged slow-flowing stream or lowland lake, or the wisdom of the sea – every water droplet's destiny? A little bit of planning for this adventure would not go amiss. Don't overstretch yourself in your early days of wild swimming. I would recommend the first few trips be short dips, somewhere you can get in and out of the water easily at the same point so that the logistics don't overwhelm you. If possible, go with an experienced wild swimmer so they can guide you through the process and help you keep it simple. This will free up the mind and help you achieve early mindfulness success.

As you plan your early swims, have a look through this checklist:

- Remember the bare essentials (unless you plan to bare all): a swimsuit, goggles and towel.
- Make sure you know how you will get to the water, if you need transport and how long the walk-in will be, if there is one.
- Check your legal right to access – it varies from country to country but in England you can swim in all tidal waters, navigable waters and traditional bathing sites.
- Weather conditions – do you need sunscreen or waterproofs for after your swim?

- Tides – if you are going in the sea, make sure you know what the tides are up to. Check out conditions with a local who knows the stretch of water to ensure rip currents are not an issue.
- If you are swimming in a colder climate the water will chill you, so take plenty of warm clothes and a flask of warm drink for after your swim.
- Swimming always makes me hungry – a good hearty cheese and chutney sandwich after a swim tastes like the best food on earth. Pack yourself a snack.
- If you are inexperienced, make sure your swimming spot is well recognized as a safe place and take someone with you who can provide physical and moral support.
- Consider a dry bag to keep everything together and dry on the bank – there's nothing more disappointing than damp clothes and food after a lovely swim.
- If you will need to walk back to your starting point, consider towing a dry bag with shoes, a thin wrap and some cash. Alternatively, ask a friend to meet you at the swim's end.
- If you are in very cold waters, consider a swim skin or even a wetsuit – it is not as much fun as feeling the water on your skin but you will be able to stay in longer.
- Mobile phone – much as it is tempting to stay out of contact, some means of communication can be reassuring, but make sure it stays clear of the water.

by the power of the water. These can be deep, dark places that the sun rarely finds, but before long they open out to daylight – a brilliant, sun-filled valley, the river spreading and shallowing to take in its new-found freedom. The water in these areas slows as it relaxes and spreads out; compared to the river in the cutting, it can be surprisingly warm. These swims are not physically distinguishable from my previous worldwide wild swimming experiences but I am now bringing a new consciousness to the water, a heightened awareness of my emotions and the physical sensations – I am more present in the moment, I am developing the art of swimming mindfully. And how much richer it is.

A Mindful Approach

If this is your first experience of swimming mindfully and in wild waters, take your time and enjoy every sensation as it develops – all the way from trepidation to elation. Be open to the experience, expect the unexpected and take things as they come.

REACHING THE WATER IS ALL PART OF THE EXPERIENCE. Make it mindful. Don't just finish a phone call on the bank and dive straight in – stop to take a moment to enjoy the transition. Savour the anticipation and make your preparations and approach into a meaningful ritual. Think about why you have chosen to swim and what steps you have taken to make space in your day for this adventure. Think about your journey here. Dwell a moment upon the water's journey here – ocean currents, river channels... As you shed your clothes, shed the stresses and constraints those clothes may signify. How does the air feel as it reaches your skin? The sensations of the skin are a large factor in the art of wild swimming and it starts while you are making your bankside preparations.

Look around you. Feel the pressures of your life ebb away as you take in the subtle tones of nature's wallpaper. Focus on the sensations on your feet as you step out of socks and shoes. How does it feel? Is it cool, or warm? Oozing mud between your toes? Sharp stones, so you want to withdraw your foot before it even touches down, or even hot granular sand?

How are you feeling? Concentrate for a few moments on your emotions – you may be excited, or you may be fearful, anxious or trepidatious, or maybe the overwhelming sensation you're feeling is one of freedom. There are so many variables to a wild swim. You haven't even touched the water yet and your senses are already singing with overload and your emotions are whirring. There is little space in your mind at this moment for all the distractions of everyday life – imagine how it will feel when you actually make it into the water.

Notice Your Breathing

As you start to focus in on the experience, take a moment to notice your breathing. Breathing is one of the most natural,

automatic actions our body undertakes – in-out, in-out – ten to twenty cycles a minute. But breathing is one of the most important actions to master for meditation and for swimming. The first instinct of our body on entering wild water is to tense up; our breathing shallows and becomes irregular, and sometimes we even forget to breathe for a bit. While this would seem to be a negative response to the water, it does mean that we are already conscious of our breathing, which provides the perfect focus for our exercise. Before we get into the water, we are going to prepare ourselves for the experience.

It is time for you to take charge and get that breathing under control – see the Mindfulness Exercise opposite.

GETTING IMMERSED

Now it's time to make your acquaintance with the water. Start off slowly. You may be lucky and start your wild swimming in the warm, crystal-clear depths of the Caribbean, with a shallow, shelving, soft sand seabed to float in on, or you may not.

THE MAJORITY OF WILD SWIMS are not so benign. They challenge the mind and body in ways you have probably not experienced before – rocky or muddy ground, invariably cool water and often slightly awkward entry and exit points. So start slowly and enjoy every challenge as it presents itself – relish the slight revulsion you first emote when you cannot

MINDFULNESS EXERCISE

AND... BREATHE

Before you get immersed in the water, you are going to get immersed in breathing. I have adapted this breathing exercise from one of Thich Nhat Hanh's; to set you on the route to mindfulness as you prepare. As you sit or stand, breathe smoothly and deeply – in through the nose and out through the mouth – saying the following couplets. Repeat the whole exercise about three times until you start to relax. You may close your eyes as you do this if you wish.

Breathing in, I'm breathing in. Breathing out, I'm breathing out.

Breathing in, deeply. Breathing out, slowly.

Breathing in, calm. Breathing out, ease.

Breathing in, smile. Breathing out, release.

Breathing in, the present moment. Breathing out, a wonderful moment.

As you repeat the phrases, focus on the key word of each couplet. Be aware of the air flooding into your body and observe how your body responds as you say the words.

As you do this exercise, you may find that thoughts bubble up – like debris caught in a river current, you can witness their arrival but try to let them pass by without being swept along. If your mind does drift, gently return to your breathing couplets as soon as you notice.

As you relax into a steady rhythm, you can return to your natural breathing pattern and open your eyes. Slowly move to the water. Try to maintain your breathing pattern as you lower yourself in.

see through the water to the bed, really live the experience of that sharp intake of breath as the less than tropical waters first lap over your ankles. Feel every sensation and log it away as a bright memory to be taken home and cherished, to bring out and dwell on when you are tucked up later by the fire.

As you first start to immerse yourself, don't worry about swimming. Just lower yourself into the water and see how it feels on the skin. Water has many temperatures and textures, but the pressure it exerts on the skin is an all-over body massage. Think about your breathing – how is the experience affecting tension around your chest and diaphragm? As this is your first time, you may feel anxious and breathless. Try to relax your shoulders, then your chest; push your shoulders back and down, and allow the air to flow smoothly into your lungs. Breathe it down deep, expanding your chest and keeping your shoulders low. Allow your breathing to settle into a comfortable rhythm; feel the sensation of the water on your skin and wriggle your feet into the ground to give yourself a good solid base. Once you have achieved a slightly more relaxed posture and a calm rhythm in your breathing, then you can think about lifting your feet from the bottom, finding your buoyancy and actually starting to swim.

Entering the Alien World

Many wild swimmers, myself included, find it hard to get their head under the water at the start of a swim. Depending

Just You and the Water

In swimming pools, we may feel we have to conform to the expected styles of swimming and become self-conscious if we stray too far from the recognized strokes. Luckily, beyond keeping yourself safe there are no rules in wild swimming – it's between you and the water. There are no lines on the bottom to follow, no sides for tumble turns and you don't get disqualified for swimming with a screw kick.

If you have a less-than-conventional swimming style, it is worth remembering that front crawl, back crawl, breaststroke and butterfly are actually very modern inventions. The earliest recognizable stroke to be employed was breaststroke, which modelled the actions of the frog; this replaced the copy of the dog, which had taken precedence until the Elizabethan Age. Breaststroke reigned supreme in Europe until the end of the nineteenth century when overarm swimming was introduced from the Americas, where it had been used for generations. So if it suits your style, go back a few centuries and make up your own mode of propulsion.

on the ambient temperature, I may never actually get fully submerged; but even in quite warm waters it may be a few minutes before I can get past my nose and ears. While we may have crawled out of the water somewhere back in our early evolution, the water environment is something quite alien to our landlocked bodies. Water flowing into our orifices really signals our entry into this alien world. However, if you find the sensation of water in your ears and nose unbearable, you may want to resort to nose clips and earplugs. Hopefully, as you get more comfortable in the water you can get used to the new sensations and begin to enjoy them.

You are now officially wild swimming; have a look around and enjoy the experience.

MEDITATIVE WATERS

So here we are, settling in; the initial roar of ecstasy and anxiety has subsided to a gentle hum. We're enjoying the setting but we still need to float free of all our mental junk mail. Let's focus in and really start to savour the meditative powers of wild waters.

NOW YOU HAVE BEGUN TO RELAX and gain control of your breathing, lift your feet from the ground, push off and get buoyant. Some people like to stretch out and begin swimming straight away, while others like to bob around for a while as they settle in – take whichever approach suits you.

Once you are swimming, you can continue to focus on your breathing. Concentrate on the physical sensations as you breathe. Feel the air expanding your lungs and diaphragm as you breathe in, and feel it bubbling through the water as you breathe out – the resistance of the water leads to a more explosive breath, so you are naturally more conscious of your breathing than when doing other activities. This is one reason why swimming provides the perfect setting in which to practise breathing meditation. Carry on with the breathing exercises you started on the bank. Remember to try to keep relaxed and keep breathing deeply and evenly.

Stimulating the Brain

There are many reasons why swimming feels like meditation and the focus on breathing is just one of them. Swimming has been shown to stimulate neurogenesis in the hippocampus – neurogenesis literally means 'birth of neurons' and is the process by which stem cells generate new neurons for the growth and development of brain tissue. The hippocampus of the brain is an area that can atrophy (waste away) during periods of chronic stress, resulting in long-term anxiety and depression. Prozac and other drugs are used to stimulate neurogenesis – but swimming has been shown to stimulate the same response in the brain.

The regular rhythm we fall into when swimming involves alternating stretch and relaxation of skeletal muscles – this

TECHNIQUE TIP
LEARNING TO BREATHE

When you are swimming with an overarm style like front crawl, you have two breathing options. Some people do trickle breathing. This is where you release the air from your lungs as a slow-trickling exhale, usually throughout the time your mouth is underwater. In this case, as you lift your head you breathe in long and deep as your mouth is above the water. As your mouth goes back under the water you exhale, again as one long stream of breath, and so the breaths go on. The alternative is known as explosive breathing. In this case, you tend to hold your breath while your mouth is submerged and then at the last moment before you turn or lift your head you exhale all the air in one hard blow – think of how the whale breathes, the explosion of air as it surfaces, shooting its fountain of spray high into the sky. This is followed immediately by a strong, deep in-breath before you hold your breath for the first part of the submerged phase of your stroke.

How you breathe is largely a personal choice. I've noticed that my breathing changes with the speed I am swimming; for a long, slow swim I tend to trickle breathe, but if I up the pace a bit then I tend to change to a more explosive style of breathing – it doesn't matter, it is personal preference. The most important thing is to find a steady rhythm and settle comfortably into it.

integral element in the skill of swimming is a primary activity in the relaxation techniques of yoga and also in many sleep techniques. This action works to loosen up any body tension, leaving you feeling relaxed but energized.

Focusing on new skills is also a great way to give the mind a rest from the often negative everyday thoughts and worries that course through our brains. This allows us to become fully absorbed and be one with the experience – leave our thinking mind behind and just be in our physical being.

How Do You Feel?

After your swim, you should really start to feel the glow and positive feelings should flood your system. The endorphins that are produced during any workout will be surging around your body, converting your pre-swim state of free-floating angst into one of post-exercise muscle relaxation. Feelings of well-being, positivity and even elation may wash over you as you stretch out on the bank.

Feelings of well-being, positivity and even elation may wash over you

Remember these emotions – try to keep them with you as long as possible, but know that whenever you swim you will always leave the water feeling better than you did when you arrived. Just knowing that those positive feelings are only a dip away can be immensely reassuring.

MINDFULNESS EXERCISE

THE MINDFUL RHYTHM

*Rhythm is one of the principle pleasures
of swimming, as well as its essence.*

FROM 'WATERLOG: A SWIMMER'S JOURNEY THROUGH BRITAIN'
ROGER DEAKIN 1943–2006,
ENGLISH WRITER & ENVIRONMENTALIST FILM-MAKER

Whichever stroke you decide to use, you need to find your rhythm to really get the most from your swim. Swimming strokes that flow smoothly and rhythmically are the most efficient. Pauses, hitches, short choppy strokes, excessive glides and stops all deplete energy and momentum from your stroke and require greater energy input to get you going again. Developing a good rhythm is particularly important in open waters, where rougher water can accentuate poor rhythm. A good rhythm is also essential as a precursor to your mindfulness practice and getting in the flow.

Breathing provides a good background rhythm on which to hang your swim, but what happens if your breathing has gone awry? Music has always been a good accompaniment to swimming and it is a nice friendly way to find a rhythm. Pick your song and work the cadence of your stroke in with the beat. Often, a song just pops into your head that seems to fit the mood or the rhythm of the day.

Let the beat dictate your breathing, then fit your arm stroke to the beat and your leg cadence will follow – enjoy the marriage of your breathing and your stroke with the beat of the music. You may even find the rhythm of the sea or river seems to fall in line too – waves and ripples tuning in to the pattern of your breathing and swimming stroke.

THE JOYS OF SPRING

Although just another part of the annual cycle, spring is seen as a new beginning, a rebirth, the yearly round starting again. Likewise, the young river starts with a spring – just one step in the water cycle, a small trickle, building as it makes its way downstream. At the start of your wild swimming journey, allow it to begin gently. There is much to anticipate in these beginnings; take the challenge and start in whichever small way suits you. Taking your first strokes as the first buds of spring break out into the light will highlight to you all the best things about swimming in spring. Look forward to a mental spring clean and leaving the water with a spring in your step.

Spring Highlights

New beginnings ~ Clear water ~ Jelly spawn
Blossom blooming ~ Garlic-scented banks

Nest-building ~ Lung-busting
Mates displaying ~ Love is in the air

Lime-green shoots ~ Lambs dancing
Red-tipped leaf buds ~ Molehills erupting

The first cuckoo ~ Curlews calling
Insects emerging ~ Swallows dive-bombing

Mayfly battle ~ Kingfishers flash
Adventure brewing ~ Swim hard to keep warm

CHAPTER TWO

THE SOLO SWIM

*Swimming alone in the exclusivity of
unbroken water is sublime. It encourages you to
consider new ideas and swim towards new territories;
you expand your horizons, face new experiences and
find new joys. The personal space gained by swimming
in the solitude of wild waters allows you to see life less
turbulently; free from stress and social pressures, the
turmoil stills, soothing mind and body. Setting off
from the shore, you lose yourself in the water
— and find yourself coming in.*

THE ADOLESCENT PHASE

◆

Adolescence is often an uncomfortable conflict between readiness to take on the world and youthful lack of experience. The only way to approach this is to face your fears. Stand up tall, celebrate your strength and vulnerability and take responsibility for yourself as you embark on the solo world.

As we continue to swim and breathe, falling into the rhythm more easily, something begins to happen. Our minds are no longer as turbulent as we swim; anchored to our breathing and rhythmic stroke, we have learned to allow the stream of thoughts to bubble to the surface and float away, observing them with interest but without feeling the need to dwell on each and every one. And with this calmer mind, our bodies are also becoming absorbed in the soothing waters. Our anxious muscle tension is seeping away, leaving in its place an increasingly relaxed and supported body position.

While our early swims were characterized by a certain uneasiness, our swimming confidence has grown so that we are fully aware of our ability to confront the wild water and enjoy the swim. We are entering our adolescent swimming phase. The desire to strike out on our own and challenge ourselves becomes overwhelming. Now is the time for a solo swim. Swimming alone is very different from swimming with others – you have no responsibilities other than for yourself

◆

We ourselves must walk the path.

FROM 'THE DHAMMAPADA'
THE BUDDHA

and no one is looking out for you either. You have complete freedom to come and go as you please, and your immersion in the wild life can be complete.

A solo wild swim can be exciting and feel a little dangerous and on the edge. As you step out into this new solo world, you may experience feelings of release and freedom – buoyant confidence. Don't be too concerned if these emotions surge wildly and turn to moments of uncertainty, feeling humble, small, alone and frightened – this is, after all, the typical turmoil of adolescent development.

Brain Pruning

Neuroscientists have discovered a phenomenon that goes on in the brain known as 'pruning'. This is when the brain undergoes a major spring clean. Superfluous information is removed to make space for all the new experiences that must follow. Pruning goes on throughout our lives but happens most extensively at three key points: as a toddler, in adolescence and in our late forties and early fifties. At these times our brains are at their lightest and looking for new experiences to fill them up again. These points are characterized by periods of emotional instability and surprising choices – we are all familiar with toddler tantrums, the moody, irrational teenager and the sports-car-buying fifty-something. This is, in fact, the perfect time to branch out and expand your horizons – make new links.

The solo swim is the time to discover more about yourself and the range of waters available for solo swimming. Heading out into the watery world and taking that wild step on your own journey inspires personal creativity and independence. This is the time for personal expression and free thinking; for finding new challenges, identifying personal preferences and developing confidence in your own person. This is a period of rapid growth and development.

Safety First

An important factor in any wild swim is safety and this becomes even more of an issue when you want to head off on your own – in your planning, consider confidence and competence. Only ever take on challenges you are sure you can meet with equal levels of confidence and competence. Although you are heading off on your own, get into the habit of telling someone where you are going and when you expect to be back. As always, the safety mantra is – if in doubt, don't.

LOSE YOURSELF IN THE WATER

Sometimes, it is satisfying to leave behind the thinking mind entirely while swimming. We are composed to a large extent of water and when we are immersed we become little more than another drop in the ocean – the body and water as one.

THE WATER THAT OPENS OUT IN FRONT OF YOU is like a blank sheet of paper – open for your influence. I once stayed on the shores of Lake Coniston in the English Lake District. We were staying on the farm that Arthur Ransome used as his setting for the *Swallows and Amazons* books. I always remember the opening paragraph with Roger tacking his way across the field, pretending he is sailing. Just past dawn every morning I walked down through that sheep-trimmed sward, the low sun just catching the mountain tops, burning golds and greens. Under the iced dew, the October grass crunched, leaving my footprints verdantly green in the glistening silver of the frosted field. We were blessed with a vanishingly rare week of clear blue skies. And I had the lake to myself.

I would keep an eye on proceedings from above the surface of the water as I swam a smooth breaststroke beneath it, trying not to disturb the flat calm. As I struck out, the water was just like a mirror – the whole world inverted. I swam through the perfect reflection of the mountain known as the Old Man of Coniston – starting at its summit, I swam down its flanks, the coppery bracken burnished by the early morning sunlight. The absence of ripples and waves meant I could swim as smoothly as a fish, every shape the same as the last, no adjustments required; the water was fast and I would sometimes feel that I was really flying. My mind was free; thoughts came and went like breezes through the trees and my body followed without any need for conscious thought. I was immersed and flowing. I felt enveloped in the water, my breathing deep and satisfying, my muscles strong, moulding the water in my hands and stroking in easy rhythm. The water held me like a hug.

Leaving the water was not as elegant as the swim. My cold, numbed feet were unresponsive, and I floundered my way through the edging pond weed, emerging like some kind of a fancy-dress Medusa – green snakes of weed dripping from head and shoulders. On the return to the house, my numbed feet added to the sensation that I was floating a foot above the ground; the post-swim adrenaline and endorphins surged through my body, creating a heady sensation of lightness, the feeling of well-being overflowing.

As the Mood Takes You

When we swim on our own, we are free from any external expectations and boundaries that others apply for us. We can play in the water and allow the swim to develop in any way the mood takes us. There is no one around to dictate to us or judge us – and we are working on our mindfulness, so we are not going to be judgemental of ourselves. Our thinking minds are therefore less likely to get involved and we can allow ourselves to be fully absorbed in the physical act of swimming. As you swim, allow yourself to be fully engaged with your body. The body is sending feedback to the brain all the time – enjoy the physical sensations of the water and physical exertion of swimming; focus on the subliminal messages and connect with your body, the whole body, as it surges through the water.

A Taste of Freedom

While we swim we feel entirely absorbed, experiencing the flow of clean water and the lightness in our head and heart. At one with the water, our bodies and minds are released onto another plane – for a moment we have found our Zen, our inner peace. Like Master Shifu in *Kung Fu Panda*, we could catch a water droplet and roll it around in our hands.

At the end of your first solo wild swim, you may be struck with a different kind of elation – you have proved yourself as an independent swimmer. You have struck out on your own, released your inner fish and moved on to a whole new level of experience. Like an adolescent leaving home for the first time, you have had a taste of freedom. This is a momentous step, so take the time to look back over your swim. What were you aware of, what were you thinking about? Did you dwell on issues that had been bothering you earlier in the day or were you lost in the moment, engaged with the swim?

TECHNIQUE TIP
STAYING ON COURSE

Swimming in wild waters raises the particular problem of swimming in the right direction. With no lines to follow under the water, how do you know you are going the right way? The first challenge is to get your head above water to have a look ahead. For breaststrokers this is not a problem, as every stroke brings you to the surface, but for front crawlers it is trickier and requires an adjustment to your swimming stroke.

The best way, if you are a front crawler, is to incorporate a look as you turn your head to breathe. This can either be fitted in after you have taken your breath, so that you breathe to the side then tilt your head forwards and have a good look before returning to your stroke, or – as I prefer to do – before you breathe. In this case, you lift your head up forwards, mouth and nose still under the water, have a good look and then turn your head to the side, catching a breath before returning to your stroke. The next time you breathe, turn to the other side to check out what is happening over there. Some people find there is not enough time in their stroke to breathe and look. If you find this a problem, you will need to alternate breathing and looking – breathe on one stroke and look on the next. Depending on how many hazards there are around you, you may have to do this every time you breathe or maybe only every few breaths.

Another problem unique to wild swimming is route finding. Once you are in the water you have a very limited sight range; a small swell or slightly wavy water can quickly obscure your sight lines.

Before you start swimming, you should have a good look at the course you plan to take and identify a few landmarks – distinctive trees, buildings or other static features on the shore; anchored boats or buoys in the water. Remember that all features need to be static and raised up above the level of the water so you can see them beyond the peaks and troughs of the waves. When you lift your head to breathe, check where your landmarks are to ensure that you are staying on course. If you are going on a long swim, it is worth noting a stopping point at the end of each set of landmarks where you can pause for a few seconds to relocate yourself and identify your next set of landmarks before you move off. If there are no easily followed landmarks then you really need to think about a support boat or kayak to keep you on track and safe from hazards

An important landmark to note is your start and finish point. Entry points can easily be obscured by marginal vegetation or other people on the shore, so just after you set off turn round and have a look at it. Have a good look at a couple of immobile features (ideally one closer to you than the other) and notice how they relate to each other – a church spire and a tree that look side by side when you are opposite your starting point, the particular shape of a rock or cliff formation at that orientation. When you return – tired, hungry and thirsty – to find your clothes, you may be very glad that you took the time to notice that tree stump looking exactly like Scooby Doo from the particular angle that identifies exactly where you entered the water, and where your picnic can be found.

FIND YOURSELF IN THE WATER

◆

As we continue to explore a whole range of wild waters, there is a great deal to discover about ourselves as swimmers and as people. Swimming alone, we become aware of our potential, developing a greater understanding of our motives and purpose, setting ourselves on our path to happiness.

IN TERMS OF OUR TECHNICAL SWIMMING ABILITIES, the more we swim the more we learn about ourselves as swimmers. Swimming in wild waters is very different from being in the pool. As we explore new waters, we discover which water we enjoy best and which settings are best for our mindfulness exercises. We may also discover we have a preference for a different stroke out in the open than in a pool. I am much stronger at front crawl than breaststroke and will rarely be seen swimming breaststroke in a swimming pool, but when I am out in the wild world I love to keep an eye on the world around me – for these moments, breaststroke is much better.

Use your solo swimming time well, as this is the perfect opportunity to learn about yourself without the distractions of others – you can be entirely selfish. As well as discovering much about your swimming preferences, you may find that being in the water mindfully allows you to experience a clarity in your life that is usually muddied by technical and human influences. This word 'influence' has strong water connotations

– literally, it means flowing in; an influent would describe a tributary flowing into the main river, or a pollutant flowing into a water course. Whatever is flowing in has an impact on the receiving body – it influences it. We are subject to many influences on our lives through the pouring in of information, whether from sources of media, the people around us or indeed our environment. We are constantly bombarded by these influences and immersing ourselves in water enables us to extract ourselves temporarily. We can give ourselves some space, calm our minds and see our lives with greater clarity.

Lose Your Inhibitions

As you swim on your own, try out different ways of swimming. Different strokes and different paces. Try to emulate the wildlife you see. Swim like a swan – no apparent movement above the water but paddling hard beneath. Try diving like ducks – bottoms up. Or go for underwater swims like the grebe – when you watch a grebe, it leaps off the surface of the water and disappears for some time; predicting its surfacing point is almost impossible. Next, have a go at swimming like that most proficient of underwater mammals – the otter. Imagine the surface of the water is the state of your mind, calm and smooth; concentrate on moving with as little disruption as possible.

Swimming alone can allow us to break out of our usual constraints. We can be constrained by our need to fit into other people's agenda and perceptions but we may also be

MINDFULNESS EXERCISE

SWIM LIKE AN OTTER

'The lovely sight of an otter spreading himself over the stones, moving with the stream, … smooth as oil under the water.'

FROM 'TARKA THE OTTER'
HENRY WILLIAMSON 1895–1977, ENGLISH NOVELIST

Freshwater otters in North America and Europe have suffered as a result of habitat loss and pollution, and in the early 1900s otter numbers fell to dangerously low levels. Conservation efforts in the last half of the twentieth century have seen wonderful revivals. The number of otters in the wild may have increased but they are still elusive animals. One of the reasons they are so hard to spot, even when present, is that they move with such fluidity and harmony with the water. Beyond a water bubble trail, there is often little more sign. See if you can emulate the otter with some ripple-free swimming.

The best place to try this exercise is on a still day on a flat river or lake with wonderful reflections on the surface of the water.

Swim breaststroke so that the only part of your body breaking the surface of the water is your head. Think of your body as pouring oil; feel the weight of the water in your hands as you pull yourself forwards; feel the flow of the water past your face – gently licking your skin as you keep your movements smooth and flowing.

Breathe out, as you glide your hands forward and kick your legs out behind you; dip your nose and mouth below the surface but keep your eyes out of the water, looking ahead and enjoying the small hillock of water that builds up in front as you glide. Keep your head as low and steady as you can, only moving enough to propel your body forwards and to lift your nose out of the water to breathe.

constrained by our own imagination and confidence. Try to take the opportunity of the solo swim to break out of those constraints. Your mindfulness practice may help you to see what is happening and allow you to take this chance to go out and find yourself. Initially, it can be hard to take advantage of the freedom that the solo swim provides – you may just repeat the swims, going religiously from A to B in the way you always have. Soon, though, you can relax into the water and make some big movements, swing your arms like a loon, laugh, cry – there's no one around to judge you. Zigzag through the water, dive and sway, use your whole body and go wild – dance like no one is watching.

A WHOLE WORLD OF WATER

Wild swimming opens up a whole world of different waters to get immersed in. Wherever you go, you will soon find yourself searching local maps for promising rivers, lakes, open-air pools, beaches and bays and falling into conversation with walkers, fishermen and other swimmers to gather information on pools with potential.

WHILE EVERY WATER AND SWIM will present its own unique characteristics, certain features of the main bodies of wild waters remain constant. A lake is always still, rivers always flowing and the sea always salty. Learn a little about the main characteristics of the key waterbodies so that you can be well prepared and have some idea of the challenges that you will face when you embark on a swim.

Remember that while you may understand the setting of a waterbody in one region and the main characteristics will remain constant, there will be local details that make every waterbody unique. The rules around public access to wild waters change from country to country and the ecology will be specific to every geographical area – climate, altitude, geology and other local influences all have an impact. Human influences can impact on water quality and physical hazards in the water; this may be due to agriculture, industry or other recreational users, such as fishermen and leisure craft etc. Whenever you reach a new area, always talk to residents or other swimmers to gain a clear understanding of the local situation before you embark on a swim.

Lakes

Reassuringly still, lakes (also incorporating pools and tarns) are entry-level wild swimming. Usually relatively benign swimming environments with limited waves and currents to challenge you, they are also filled with freshwater, which doesn't make you gag when it splashes in your mouth. The fresh and relatively smooth waters of a lake will provide the closest conditions in the wild to pool swimming; with a long reach of open water, you can have a good stretch out, free from concerns and free of charge.

The main feature to be wary of in lakes is temperature. We think of water as being fluid and homogenous but it is not; the bonds in water mean that layers of water tend to stick together. In summer, the surface layer of a lake warms up, often reaching temperatures of up to 18–20°C (64–68°F); it becomes less dense and floats above the colder, deeper layers, receiving more of the sun's rays and further increasing in temperature and decreasing in density. The temperature change between layers becomes more and more distinct. If you jump into a lake or dive down, you will be sharply aware of a layer where there is a rapid drop in temperature. This layer is called the thermocline and often drops, over the depth of about a metre (3 feet), from 18°C (68°F) to 7°C (45°F). The deepest parts of a lake can drop down to 4°C (39°F), even in summer.

In winter, lakes experience a temperature inversion. This is because the density of water changes at 4°C (39°F), when it starts becoming less dense – one of nature's miracles that allows life to persist in the depths in even the coldest climates and under ice. For the swimmer, this means that in the middle of winter the depths of the lake are still at a relatively benign 4°C (39°F), while the surface waters will be 3°C (37°F), or below.

You will also encounter bands of cooler and warmer water as you swim. These are the result of inflowing streams, which tend to stay as a distinct body of water rather than mixing quickly with the receiving water. You will feel the influence of their different temperatures even some way out into the lake.

Reservoirs and pools in quarries are basically man-made lakes and follow the same rules of physics. The additional potential hazards of steep banks and man-made structures – mining debris, dams, towers, aerators, inlet, outlet – must be taken into consideration and avoided. In many countries, swimming in quarries and reservoirs is common practice (USA and Europe), while in others it is often discouraged (UK). Take note of signs and follow instructions where they are given.

Rivers

My personal favourite for wild swimming; rivers provide freshwater excitement in a huge range of conditions. From long swim safaris to small pools, rope swings and seasonal wildlife, the linear nature of rivers can make for logistical challenges but at least gives little option for getting lost. The variety and complexity of rivers is always energizing and there is always a river to suit your wild swimming mood, with just the right balance of excitement and security.

The greatest safety consideration in rivers is fast water. Following heavy rain, a river can more than double in size. The type of catchment and the position of the river in the catchment influences how quickly rainwater affects its flow. In mountainous areas, rainwater finds its way to the river quickly – the level rises rapidly within a few hours but returns to normal rapidly too; this is called a 'flashy' river. Further down the catchment and in lowland rivers, it can take a couple of days for the rainwater to reach the river. The flood will rise slowly but may stay high for considerably longer. It is best to avoid swimming in rivers in flood for a number of reasons: water quality will be considerably worse as waste and debris is washed into the rivers, unexpected currents can develop around flooded features, and the faster speed of the water may catch you unawares.

Similarly, you should avoid areas of white water as these require specialist skills. White water can be seen on rivers where the gradient increases and the water speeds up, causing disruption in the surface so that the water literally looks white. The underwater turmoil is caused by the increased speed of the water as it flows over submerged rock features – whirlpools, eddies and dangerous underwater currents can form that, if large enough, are able to trap a swimmer.

Tacked on to the end of rivers are estuaries. The twice-daily ebb and flow of the tides into and out of a river mouth allows for power swimming and wonderful opportunities for a free ride. Linking freshwaters and saline waters, estuaries are the swimming nether world, places where sediment is dropped by the outgoing river and the incoming sea estuaries are full of nutrient-rich muds and the wildlife that goes with them. Harbours are often located in the mouth of estuaries, which are invariably navigable waters – therefore, boat traffic can be an issue, so you may want to think carefully about a boat escort when you swim. Make sure you are visible to boat traffic and stay well out of the way of water-skiing areas and any busy channels generally. A certain amount of planning is required, both swimming and logistical, to make sure you catch the tide going the right way. Timing is everything – not a swim for the impulsive swimmer.

Seas

Playing in the sea will be many people's first experience of wild waters. The sights and sounds of the beach, children and dogs, catching waves in the pounding surf, salty buoyant waters – these are strongly evocative memories for many of us. Striking out from the shore for a wild swim opens up a whole new set of experiences. Quite distinct from any other swimming experience, we are really at the mercy of nature when we swim in the sea – the push and pull of the water on our buoyant bodies, moving with the swell. Considerable thought is required if you are contemplating anything more than a simple parallel shore swim on a lifeguarded beach.

Particular hazards – which change and need consideration for every stretch of coastline and before every swim – include weather, tides, waves and currents (particularly rip currents – a strong, often narrow, offshore current, which can form on any beach with breaking waves).

There are so many adventures to be had off the shore: bays and headlands, offshore islands, arches and coves to be explored – swims can be as challenging as you wish. Serious planning is

TECHNIQUE TIP
DEALING WITH WAVES AND SWELLS

Waves and rough water do not really exist in indoor pools. When you bring your swimming-pool style of front crawl to open waters, you quite often find that your hands are knocked down as you skim the water surface to reach forward for your next stroke. This can knock you off rhythm and leave you with a much shorter, less powerful stroke. Adapt to the conditions by recovering with a much higher stroke than you would use in a pool – initially it seems less efficient, but in rougher water ends up more effective than having your hand knocked down every couple of strokes. Aim higher and avoid the knock-down.

If you are swimming in the sea it is not much fun swimming in the breaking waves, so you need to get out past the breakers to find the calmer water. Sometimes this can be a challenge. As you swim out off the beach, you need to avoid being washed back to shore. Do this by diving over small waves and swimming in the gaps between them or diving under bigger waves to the deeper, still water and swim there. Remember to save a bit of breath in case you come up in the middle of a wave and have to dive straight back down again. Once you are past the breakers, you can swim along the shore in the calmer water.

Returning to shore is a bit easier because you can use the action of the waves to surf in. Try to catch the wave at its crest to use its energy to carry you in – in front of the crest or behind it, you won't get the benefit of the energy. Tuck your fingers into fists and link your thumbs as you hold your hands out in front of you to avoid banging your head or hurting your fingers if there are other people in the water with you.

required to check out the local conditions and a support boat may be advisable if you want to take on a bigger challenge. I would strongly suggest swimming in the company of an experienced local or taking local advice if you are going into unknown waters. Be realistic about your capabilities and only swim within your levels of competence.

Open-air Pools

While not strictly wild waters, open-air pools are something of a halfway house for the wild swimmer. Many open-air pools have been closed but strong communities of swimmers have developed in some areas, petitioning to keep their pool open and in some cases actually taking on its running. This strong community element tends to run through the open-air pool culture and it does not take many visits to one pool before you recognize and become recognized, gradually being absorbed into the local open-air pool culture.

Open-air pools share some of the wild water elements of chill and open-air enjoyment, without fully incorporating the wildlife and natural unpredictability of a wild swim. You can enjoy the ravages of the climate without having to suffer the nettle stings and mud to quite the same extent. The water is generally less chlorinated than indoor pools and is sometimes sourced from local springs, rivers or in coastal areas direct from the sea. To top it all, cafés and warm showers are usually readily available on site.

THE LAZY HAZE OF SUMMER

❖

The year is cycling on and the plants and animals are going through rapid growth. Life and luxuriance is all around us. On our swimming journey, we are experiencing new challenges on every trip and finding new skills to meet our needs. Like the plants and animals in summer, we are flourishing. The water on its journey is also working hard. Rushing to find its level in the sea, the river is heading downhill, forming chasms, gorges and bends; plunging into pools and carrying its load as it descends.

We are now at the peak growth in our mindful swimming development. Look around you and enjoy the abundance and richness of the summer season as you share the rich fruits of wild swimming with family and friends.

Summer Highlights

Life and laughter ~ Warm sandy beaches
Shimmer and sparkling waves ~ Grasshoppers chirp

Dragonflies zither ~ Bats flicker ~ Life's full and blowsy
Sleepy and scented ~ A colour mosaic of floral proportions

Flies waltz and insects hum ~ Swallows swoop and chatter
Long rosy evening glow ~ Mowing meadows ~ Dewy mornings

Sleeping under the stars ~ Dawn chorus ~ Morning mists
Relaxing on the bank ~ Lush margins ~ Heat haze

Trees fully dressed ~ Luxuriant growth
A floral riot ~ Desiccated land

CHAPTER THREE

SWIMMING
WITH FRIENDS

*Water bonds us, dissolving barriers and
diluting differences. As we shed our clothes, we
drop our pretensions; classless and ageless, we slip
into egalitarian camaraderie. Braving the elements
with friends expands the joy; the water washes away
tensions and provides the medium for fun and laughter
to dominate the day — the euphoria and pride on your
companions' faces reflects your own emotions and
amplifies the experience. As you grow fast into your
wild swimming and mindfulness skills, enjoy the
richness of life and share it with friends.*

WATER BONDS

◆

Water is so ubiquitous that we rarely give it a second glance. The Ancient Greek philosopher Aristotle labelled it as an element, along with fire, earth and air, but only recently have we come to understand that without water there really would be no life.

THE SIMPLE MOLECULE FORMED OF ONE HYDROGEN and two oxygens that defies all scientific norms is the matrix and medium through which all other molecules can become something useful. Every living entity on our planet is made up of at least 50 per cent water. We ourselves start life suspended in the womb with a composition of up to 95 per cent water, dropping to 77 per cent at birth and slowly desiccating throughout our lives to 60 per cent in old age. Rather than visualizing ourselves as vessels containing water, we are more like the gelatinous creature B.O.B. in *Monsters versus Aliens* — waterbodies containing dissolved or suspended nitrogen, carbon, hydrogen, oxygen, phosphorus and sulphur. It is no wonder then that suspending ourselves in water can feel so delightfully reassuring and welcoming.

If water complied with the usual chemical rules, it would be entirely unremarkable; but happily it makes up its own rules. At the molecular scale, water is like a miniature magnet — the hydrogen atoms are minutely positively charged and the oxygen atoms minutely negatively charged. These charges

create an attraction, a strong bond between the molecules, which accounts for much of water's unique nature. As a start, greater energy is required to break water molecules apart than other liquids of similar sized molecules, which means we have liquid water in our atmosphere. Water, by rights, should only exist as a vapour – there shouldn't even be any wild water on our planet for us to swim in.

Life Support

All liquids have a linear relationship between temperature and density – the density increases as they cool. However, water suddenly diverts from this at 4°C (39°F) and starts to reduce in density. This means that colder water floats and ice forms on the surface of water. This simple change is essential for life on Earth. Deeper layers of water at the base of rivers and lakes remain unfrozen during winter at temperatures of more than 4°C (39°F), allowing life to survive throughout the year in all regions of the world.

These stronger bonds also result in what we know of as surface tension, a kind of skin that forms on the surface of water; capillary action, which draws liquids up narrow tubes; and also a disproportionate lack of compressibility. Without its strong bonds, trees could not draw water and nutrients up into their leaves, bugs could not walk on water, blood would not flow in our veins and we would not be able to operate our water supply systems.

Building Bonds with People

But water does not just create bonds at the molecular level – it also acts as a bonding agent for people. While studying sports massage therapy, I learned about the importance of the skin – the largest organ in the body. Massaging the skin is well known to evoke feelings of well-being and happiness. These emotions are caused by the flood of oxytocin released when the skin is massaged. Oxytocin, also known as the bonding or hug hormone, is very important in parent–baby bonding and romantic attachment in adults. Swimming in water has much the same effect as a massage. The whole-body contact with the water as you swim massages the skin, releasing the same oxytocin into the system – bringing about feelings of calm and pleasure and increasing empathy and trust and therefore engendering good relationships with those around you. It may be the reason that immersion in water has strong sensuous and romantic connotations.

The buoyancy and density of water changes the way we move. When we are suspended in water, we are physically supported; the movements we make against the heavy water become slow and smooth even if we try to make them harsh and fast. Muscle tension is reduced. Anger and aggressions are hard to sustain when we are immersed in water, which absorbs the physical responses required. Water is a great soother in many ways; there can be no calmer and happier place to be with our family and friends.

Taking on a new challenge is a wonderful experience; facing the excitement and euphoria, the pitfalls and achievements with others is a great way to get to know someone in a new setting. When we do this, we encounter our companions in a way we haven't before; we see them through new eyes and feel very close to one another. Carrying out an activity can be a great icebreaker and shared experiences quickly build bonds.

SHED YOUR SKIN

◆

As we peel off our clothes for a swim, we shed a layer of our identity, along with the labels and pretensions they portray. Freedom from our daily uniform allows us to celebrate what unites us as a human race, rather than focusing on what divides us.

WHEN WE GET DRESSED IN THE MORNING, our clothes have a big impact on our frame of mind and also how we portray ourselves for the day ahead. Like it or not, our clothes send out signals about who we are and what we are doing. I encourage my children to be smartly dressed and wear suitably uncomfortable shoes for school, when they would rather wear Vans or Converse, because I believe they will be judged on their appearance and I also believe looking smart puts them in the right frame of mind to work well. Unfortunately, the clothing we wear can divide us into social groups and create barriers that can be difficult to cross.

Swimming provides us with a unique, socially acceptable opportunity to break through those social barriers, liberating us from the shackles of our clothing and the expectations and the persona they encourage us to portray.

WOW!

The one barrier that can prevent people from swimming is concern over their bodies. It is not often that we are in a state of near undress with people we know and love, let alone in front of complete strangers. So much of today's media is focused around how we look and since very few of us are blessed with Elle 'The Body' Macpherson proportions, the prospect of baring almost all can be off-putting. However, we really do come in all shapes, sizes and colours; our lives have etched our experiences indelibly on our bodies and we should bear them with pride. If you want to read a celebration of all your body has been through, take a look at Hollie McNish's poem 'WOW!' – our bodies tell our life stories and if we can learn to love them enough to get into the water, then that is sufficient. Once you decide to take the plunge, you will be surprised how quickly you become comfortable with the idea.

I have found no other activity that breaks down the social barriers like swimming. It is hard to be pompous or superior or judgemental in any way when you are in your swimsuit. The vulnerability of near nakedness exposes our humanity and the shared empathy it creates is enlightening.

SHARING THE EXPERIENCE

◆

The support and companionship we gain from wild swimming with others provides much more than added safety. The camaraderie and shared experience accentuates the feelings of well-being and happiness while on the swim and allows the memory to live on beyond the scope of the day.

As we swim mindfully with others, we break down the barriers between us. There develops a wonderful shared experience with our fellow swimmers that fosters feelings of connectedness and togetherness. We are unified and more aware, closer to our companions and able to relate to them better. Our previous mindfulness practice has helped us to develop an understanding of ourselves, but it can sometimes feel a bit self-absorbed; however, when we use mindfulness to observe what is going on, to find acceptance of our inner workings and go with our flow, we become happier and more balanced and we then have the capacity to direct our interests beyond our self. As you notice your emotions and sensations, expand your awareness to take in those around you.

Take a moment to notice how your fellow swimmers are getting on. Your companions may be having a great time or they may be lost in their own battles – fatigue, hunger, pain, solitude can all strike at any time. Keep your eyes open and be alert to your fellow swimmers' state of mind and body and

A Cure for the Grumps

It starts with the walk in. Before we even get out of the car I'm grumpy. It's been quite a challenge getting out of the house this evening, probably due to my poor planning, and I'm not about to let a nice swim get in the way of a good grump.

As we walk along, the deepening blue sky and still warm air can't dispel the depths of my mood. Head down, I stomp on, the others chatting quietly, trying hard to ignore my moody huffs and puffs. When we reach the sand, the huffs and puffs continue as we wriggle out of clothes, fiddling with goggles, trying to keep the sand in our clothes to a minimum. We are planning to swim up the coast for a couple of miles and then either swim or walk back, depending on our mood.

As we walk into the shallows, I'm still fiddling with my goggles and haven't managed to see anything beyond my small, tight, grumpy bubble. Suddenly, breaking through my close focus, Paul says, 'Look at the sun on the waves.' I actually do, and it is as if a door has been opened. I feel the fresh breeze on my tight forehead and playing around my hunched shoulders, which drop about a foot. I feel the soft ridges of the sand beneath my feet. I hear the light hiss and run of the gently breaking waves lapping over the sand and shingle, and I see the most beautiful dancing fairy lights, silver and gold, scattered in a trail heading out towards the setting sun. An enchanted diamond carpet leading us

out into the water. Suddenly I am transformed; my mood has lifted and I can finally enjoy this magical evening. As we wade into the water, out of nowhere a head pops out of the waves, and then a couple more. Surveying us calmly with their large, watery brown eyes, shiny black heads and whiskery noses is a small group of grey seals out for their evening swim.

The six of us are in stalemate for a couple of minutes, frozen in mid action. Three humans, thigh deep in the surf, three seals bobbing in the swell, everyone alert, waiting for the first move. The sun dazzles and sparks off the waves around the seals as if they are in a firework display, oystercatchers run peeping up and down the strand line, the breeze plays in our hair – and still we stand, the water tugging at our legs like an impatient child. Come and play! In a smartly choreographed move, the three seals turn as one and dive under an incoming wave. They swim swiftly up the coast; we see a couple of backs breaking the surface and one of them pops up a head to look back – and they are gone. The spell is broken and we all start chatting and laughing, moving into the water again to start our swim. Overjoyed at our encounter with the seals. Gradually, the spirit of the evening seeps in, my mood floats away, and I am transformed again – all smoothed out and enjoying my swim.

be ready to intervene if required. A simple kind word or a friendly observation may make the difference between your companion having a good or bad experience.

Safety in Numbers

Staying mindful is also necessary for safety. Wild swimming in a group is invigorating and exciting – if you have ever come across a group of friends swimming in a river, lake or sea, there is always a lot of noise. It is very easy to get caught up in

---

TECHNIQUE TIP
SWIMMING WITH SEALS

Swimming alone, you may find yourself exposed to all manner of wildlife that would normally run a mile if you walked up to it on the bank. We are not seen as a threat in the same way when we are in the water. Most wildlife is considerably smaller than we are and probably won't worry you, but one animal you may be lucky enough to encounter is the seal. Insatiably curious and wonderful to swim with, seals can be quite alarming, purely because of their size. There are many aspects of seals that are quite dog-like. Facially, they appear very similar to a Labrador and, like dogs, they tend to use their mouths to explore new objects and apparently have a similar level of intelligence. Seals are rarely aggressive to humans, so as with dogs remain calm and confident and you may be treated to a wonderful swimming experience. Whatever you do, relish your encounter with seals – grey seals are internationally rare, with fewer remaining globally than the African elephant.

the excitement of the moment and lose your awareness of those around you. Remember to keep a weather eye on others and if you are going on a long swim, make sure you all buddy up and keep an eye on each other to ensure you take the whole group along with you and that no one gets left behind.

We bring out the best in each other when we work together for a joint goal, and the greatest pleasure of a day swimming with friends is that the day extends beyond the water. There's nothing better after a lovely wild swim than to be able to sit down with a drink and some food and talk through the experience with someone who was there. Reliving the highs and the lows amplifies our enjoyment of the experience and allows it to live on longer.

MAKING MEMORIES

While much of life merges into an indistinct blur, the brightly jewelled memories of wild waters glint and sparkle, enduring vividly, often related to time away from the everyday routines of work and school – high days and holidays, festivals and feast days, family days and feel-good days.

I T IS WITHIN OUR NATURE TO CONGREGATE around water. Reaching back in time to our early civilizations, when daily survival was based around access to water, man developed a reverence for it, eventually lifting up deities and celebrating

and revering water. Modern-day religions have dropped the water deities but incorporated water into daily rituals and routines. Throughout cultures from the Maya and Ancient Egyptians to modern-day Judaism, Christianity and Islam, water features in rituals of birth, life and death. In the secular world, waterside weddings and the scattering of ashes over water are both regularly performed. Water is a great medium for meaningful moments throughout our lives and it is the perfect choice if you want to gather your family and friends and create some memories.

A Watery Farewell

A large group of us gathered to send off our good friends on a six-month family adventure to New Zealand. There were around nine families with twenty-five or so children ranging from sixteen down to two. Blessed with a rare warm, sunny day, we headed to the base of the Langstrath Valley in Cumbria where the river plunges off the river plain down through a series of small cataracts, water pools and rock chutes. The walk out takes about an hour and we ambled slowly, chatting, mixing and merging as we went, laden down with swimming accoutrements, packed lunches and draped children. The top of the cataracts provides the perfect staging area; a braided river, shallow channels over smooth gravel beds, and sheep-cropped banks merging gently with the water. We could lounge out and eat and chat and paddle in safety.

MINDFULNESS EXERCISE

ENJOY THE MOMENT

Swimming with other people can be great fun – but it is also easy to let life pass you by.

In among the business of a day, try to stop for a moment and notice what is going on. Be open to the sensations of your body and mind. Notice what others are doing and try to imagine what they are feeling and sensing – put yourself into their bodies and minds.

When we pause, we allow ourselves to be firmly in the present; it cements our emotions and sensations into our memory. When we try to put ourselves into another person's skin, we gain greater awareness of the moment and a greater empathy for others, seeing the world with different eyes. Don't keep this awareness to yourself. Say something to someone you are with – ask them to feel how the water is on their skin or identify a smell. A simple comment can help them really capture the essence of wild swimming.

Explore with all your senses, and notice what you have never noticed before about being in water. What memories does it evoke? Which people come into your mind (if any)? How does it make you feel? Are they all positive emotions?

Remember to try to notice your emotions and sensations without judgement. Don't expect every memory to be sparkling and wonderful. It is okay to have bad memories – they are as much 'us' as our good memories. Bad memories and anger are real emotions and part of what makes us human; they should not be brushed aside. By acknowledging they exist, we can negate some of the power they may hold over us – they can no longer control us. Be kind to yourself and you may find you become kinder and less judgemental of others.

Just downstream, though, was the most amazing series of pools. The river rapidly disappears between 5-metre (16-foot)-high cliffs, forming the most beautiful pools of limpid aquamarine blues and greens. The water is so clear you can see right down to the bottom of the pools; silvery dashes indicated the presence of fish down in the depths. There were dramatic and challenging jumps all the way around this deep pool and everyone found their own level to jump from – you just had to, it was too inviting. The smaller kids had just a small step to jump off, while the older kids and adults could challenge themselves with up to 8-metre (26-foot) jumps into the pool. Many hours were spent in plucking up courage – surrounded by a noisy cauldron of support from watching friends. The exhilaration, excitement and camaraderie were wonderful.

Along with the jumping, there was good swimming to be had; starting upstream of the pool, you could swoosh down a bubbling water chute, swim fully suspended through the invisible water, and about 50 metres (55 yards) downstream you were treated to another series of huge water chutes. Big, wide slabs of exposed rock over which the river flows, forming the best water slides you can imagine – all ending in another series of pools for gentle swimming and wallowing. We spent the whole day there, fully absorbed in our wild swimming experience, invigorated, living and loving every moment. As a family, we regularly relive the memory of this wonderful day, recalling the invigorating sensations and warm emotions.

Finding Silence

At some point in the day all the fun, excitement and noise may become too much. The great part about wild swimming is that solitude is only a dip below the surface away. Any time you crave a few moments alone, all you have to do is duck your head beneath the surface and you are again alone with the water. Swim a few strokes and take yourself away from the crowd. Lie back in the water, hear the scritch of the underwater world, calm your mind and be still. When we take a few moments out of the whirlwind and just breathe, our relationship with the world and our surroundings changes just a little bit. We can see it more clearly and enter it more fully. Standing back from the group, we can now observe our setting more carefully; we can see the patterns of relationships and re-enter the fray with greater consideration.

A Synonym for Remembering

The Vietnamese Buddhist monk, peace activist and author Thich Nhat Hanh says that the 'opposite of mindfulness is forgetfulness', which suggests that mindfulness is a synonym for remembering. When we carry out an activity mindfully, we will remember it much better than if we just let it wash over us. When we experience the mindful art of wild swimming with friends, we have the perfect recipe for creating great and lasting memories that will never be forgotten.

Enjoy the richness of life and share it with friends as you grow fast into your wild swimming and mindfulness skills. The water environment provides something for everyone in a large group – intensely invigorating and exciting as well as calming and relaxing. For those who want to sit on the bank and soak up the scene, that is one option; and for those who want the excitement and euphoria of playing in the water, that is also available. Groups of friends in the water are always splashing and laughing, setting each other new challenges and inciting silliness. Along with the naturally buoyant nature of water, these all lift the spirits and provide additional bonding opportunities between friends.

Whether for a special celebration or just for a quiet swim with friends and family, the water environment will enhance the occasion, building profound and lasting memories. Take a moment to bring to mind your own experiences in, on or beside a river, lake or sea.

MINDFULNESS EXERCISE

FLYING PRACTICE

✳

*The next most lovely thing was that
the Wart had no weight. He was not earth-bound
any more and did not have to plod along on a flat surface,
pressed down by gravity and the weight of the atmosphere.
He could do what men have always wanted to do, that is, fly.
There is practically no difference between flying in the water
and flying in the air.... It was like the dreams people have.*

FROM 'THE ONCE AND FUTURE KING'
T.H. WHITE 1906–64, ENGLISH NOVELIST

At first, the sensation of wild waters on your body may feel unnatural and you may tense up, so that your movements start out all crunched up and small. As you acclimatize to the water and take control of your breathing, feel your body loosen and relax; your movements become bigger and freer and you soon find you can float and move around with confidence. Take a moment to revel in your new-found confidence. Swoosh your arms from side to side, sway your body, feel the pressure of the water on your limbs, push against it with your hands. Bob down in the water and raise and lower your arms like a bird flying. Enjoy the sensations of weightlessness – float and hover, dive and swoop, feel the freedom you are developing. Expand beyond the restrictions within your mind and grow into the water around you. Be open to the watery world, fully immersed.

The pressure of the water gives your skeleton a rest as it supports your body in a state of weightlessness. We feel as if we weigh less when in the water. Think about how these changes are benefiting you in terms of stress on the body and stress in your mind.

CHAPTER FOUR

SWIMMING ADVENTURES

The innate desire to explore and discover new places is deeply ingrained in the human condition — generations before us have tested themselves in the wild and the success of our species has relied on this driving force. Adventures push us to our limits, allowing us to grow beyond all our expectations. On our return, we are overflowing with the experience — physically and mentally tired, but with our souls enlightened and our spirits rejuvenated.

THE CALL OF THE WILD

◆

Standing on the brink of a river, lake or sea, gazing off to the distant horizon, it is hard not to be drawn into an adventure – to see what is around the next corner and uncover the mysteries of the world.

As a six-year-old, I camped on the shores of a Swedish lake with my family. Every day we swam and went fishing, cooking our food on the shore and being eaten by midges in the process. I was a confident swimmer (an aspirational fish) and was enjoying splashing around our beach, clambering on the rocks and generally exploring. However, my brothers, aged thirteen and eleven, had spotted a bigger adventure. Across the other side of the lake, some elephantine grey rocks loomed up among the conifers, casting mysterious shadows over the dark waters of the deepest depths. Intent on a man-sized adventure, my brothers struck out towards the furthest margins.

I watched them go, slowly getting smaller and smaller, pink arms cartwheeling, flicks of spray marking their position until eventually they clambered out and flopped onto the rocks, sunning themselves like stranded starfish. It looked inviting and I was convinced I could go too. I strode out into the water with conviction in my heart but my mother, wise to the look in my eye, called me back. After lengthy and heated debate, my ambitions were quashed – my mother was no killjoy, but she had good reason. Although confident in my

swimming, and ardent in my desire to find adventures, I was possibly not as competent as I wanted to believe. I recall we had borrowed a cork belt from our Swedish friends to help with my buoyancy. I was much offended by this item.

Ready for the Next Step

So that was me at the age of six on the side of a big lake – I was entirely unconscious of my incompetence and ready to strike out into the unknown. As adults, we have bitten into the apple from the tree of knowledge. We suffer from all manner of insecurities and personal doubts; we are all too aware of our limitations and the competence we may lack. However, the pleasure in learning a new skill mindfully is to be personally aware, to measure and relish our improving skills and increased competence. As we progress, we reach the realization that we now have the skills to tackle some greater challenges.

Adventures can come in all shapes and sizes, but the main consistent features combine a physical challenge with a mental challenge, with some element of uncertainty or unknown in

---

Twenty years from now you will be more
disappointed by the things you didn't do than by the
ones you did do… Explore. Dream. Discover.

FROM 'P.S. I LOVE YOU'
H. JACKSON BROWN JR., AMERICAN AUTHOR

the mix. The very fact that you are heading into wild waters brings the vagaries of nature into the equation and almost guarantees an adventure.

Planning is very important for safety in wild swimming but be prepared to leave some sense of the unknown or else the adventure is lost. When you get the safe framework in place, you can incorporate a bit of spontaneity or make adjustments to go with the flow of the day. With the right frame of mind, any swim can be a mini-adventure and it can be squeezed into the smallest gap, even in a busy working week.

Dream Bigger

The psychological benefits of a little adventure in our lives are huge – it can enlighten our soul. Adventures encourage us to step outside our comfort zones and challenge ourselves, keeping us mentally sharp and physically strong. Overcoming challenges helps us to develop our confidence and feeds our curiosity. Adventures then become self-perpetuating – each one leaves us wanting more. Every adventure changes us in some way, however small. They encourage us to become more confident in ourselves and our abilities – to dream bigger.

The other great thing about an adventure is that it can interrupt our everyday flow – this breaks into our comfortable rhythm of life and forces us to notice something extraordinary. The more adventures we fit into our lives, the longer our lives will seem. The reason time appears to speed up when we get

MINDFULNESS EXERCISE

FEEL THE BURN

At some point in your adventure, you may find that you want or need to push yourself really hard physically, to achieve that gratifying sense of elation caused by the expression of physical strength and the achievement of the swimming rhythm – the formation of a purely spontaneous smile.

Always try to start your swim gently, settling into a rhythm and warming up your muscles gradually to reduce the risks of injuring yourself. Concentrate on the ebb and flow of your breath; enjoy the synchronicity of movements as they fit together perfectly into a relaxed, controlled stroke.

When you feel ready, up your pace.

Pull harder and reach further with your arms; speed up your leg kick. Concentrate on the sensations you feel as the muscles tense in your back and shoulders as you pull – try to keep your neck long and relaxed. Accelerate your arms to the end of the stroke. Feel the pressure of the water as it resists your pull; get hold of that water and shoot it out behind you as you surge forwards. Draw your breaths in deep and fast and expand your chest as far as possible to accommodate them. Feel the strength in your core muscles as you hold them strong, providing the stability off which the shoulders and hips can work their magic.

You should start to feel the heat in your muscles as they work hard – this is the burn. Try to focus on the sensations in your muscles and your deep strong breaths as you aim to relax the muscles that don't need to be working and maintain the tension in those that do.

Feel the unbridled joy at the strength in your body as you work smoothly and efficiently, powering through the water.

older is that we tend to repeat the same patterns day in, day out, so that every day merges into the next; everything feels familiar and unremarkable. When we were young, time went on forever because every day was an adventure, so many of our experiences were new and exciting. By inserting more adventures into our lives, we can make time stretch out again.

SWIMMING IN WATERFALLS

A waterfall is the ultimate rush. Ribbons of molten glass stream down the rock face, bouncing and exploding into shards of spray, catching and sparking light. A maelstrom of sight and sound, invigorating and exciting the senses until you are organically involved in the scene.

As a student travelling around Australia, some friends and I were on a long, dusty, hot walk in the Northern Territories and decided to stop for a swim in a remote waterhole. Across the far side of the pool, a waterfall like a giant mare's tail cascaded down the high rock face. We swam around in the pool for some time and then, drawn to the crashing waterfall, headed out to investigate. As I reached the edge of the spray, the water stung me like hailstones. Distracted by this, I took another step forward and the ground disappeared from beneath my feet. The water pummelled the top of my head and I was pushed under the surface by the sheer force. As my shock subsided, I allowed myself to slip below the surface and swam away. I stood watching the waterfall, puffing and panting with renewed awe and understanding. I would be more prepared another time and wow! Now I understood how canyons, river cliffs and all those beautifully smooth, sculpted river-hewn rock features were formed.

TECHNIQUE TIP
SPEEDING UP

There are three main elements of your stroke to work on if you want to swim faster.

1. Reach as far forward as you can at the start of your stroke to maximize the length of your underwater pull.

2. To get the most power out of that arm, accelerate hard to the end of the push past your hips, flicking the water out behind you. I was always taught that 75 per cent of your power comes from the last 25 per cent of your arm pull. I don't know if the numbers are exactly right, but you can feel the power this generates in the rush of the water past your ears.

3. Focus on your kick. In front crawl distance swimming, you typically have a very relaxed leg kick with a cycle of one or two kicks per arm cycle. The legs provide little power, just balancing the stroke. When you speed up, the kick cycle increases until you are kicking at around eight kicks per arm cycle and these kicks are much more powerful and meaningful, providing a significant impact to your speed.

Combine the long, hard arm pull with increased kick frequency and you will find you are powering through the water as if you had a motor on your heels.

A Little Too Much Adventure

After a while, we swam over to the waterfall cliff and climbed up to look back into the pool – only to see, practising star floats in the water, three crocodiles. Horrified, we stared open-mouthed at the pool, shocked that we had been swimming with these creatures. To avoid swimming back through the pool to regain our clothes, we now had to scale the rock face that the waterfall was hammering down and walk half a mile through the Australian bush in our bare feet and underwear. As we finally hobbled our way back to our waiting shoes and clothes, we met a couple just preparing to jump into the pool themselves. We warned them that we had just seen crocodiles in the pool and had escaped up the waterfall, and described our epic walk back round. They looked at us as if we were mad, said 'They're only freshies', and promptly dived into the water and swam off. Leaving us, again, open-mouthed and speechless. The kookaburra sitting in the old gum tree cackled loudly, having a good laugh at our expense that day.

There is much beautiful wildlife to see when you are in and around the water and very often it will be less fearful of you while you are submerged. When we swim in the wild, we feel a part of nature and begin to get to know the world we inhabit. There are relatively few dangerous animals in the water but it is always worth being well-informed about the local wildlife and approaching new experiences with sufficient curiosity and intelligence.

Be Crocwise

The freshwater crocodiles of Northern Australia are generally harmless to humans. Unlike their more dangerous saltwater relatives, they have a narrow snout and smaller teeth and are smaller – an adult male rarely exceeds 3 metres (10 feet). By contrast, saltwater crocodiles are highly aggressive predators and fully grown males regularly reach 6 metres (20 feet). They will take any food that enters their territory, including humans and can be found extensively in Northern Australia, Guinea and India – crucially they don't restrict themselves to saltwater. To learn more, see the website Be Crocwise.

Approach with Caution

Every wild swim reveals some new nugget of information that adds to our understanding and acceptance of the natural world. When encountering new species in the wild, always show them some respect – they would usually much rather not be around you and will invariably move away as you approach. And when approaching falling water, just remember the forces that are involved – 1 litre (2 pints) of water weighs 1 kilogram (2 pounds) and 1 cubic metre (1¼ cubic yards) of water weighs 1 tonne, and if that is falling under the force of gravity it can cause some damage. If you want a massage, stick with very low waterfalls – otherwise you will be in for a pummelling.

SWIMMING IN THE RAIN

The first instinct when it starts to rain is to run for cover. The same instinct strikes us when we are in the water, but then comes the realization — I'm swimming, I'm already wet, I don't need to shelter. It's a strangely rewarding fact that brings a goofy smile to your face.

THE BILLOWY CLOUDS CHANGE and with it the mood of the day. They darken in the centre, as if having grey watercolour dripped into them and the margins glow with contrasting light — the silver lining. The clouds congregate, thickening and converging, silent flocks heading in to roost. The breeze comes next, raising ripples on the water surface, disrupting the reflections and sending shards of light in all directions. We don't have long to wait until the first fat, heavy drops of rain plop into the water, releasing a kaleidoscope of rings that spread across the surface. The drops get smaller and faster, pockmarking the surface now in a frenzy of mismanaged acne. We shriek in excitement, splashing the water up into a turmoil of spray and delight — warm rain and cold spray merge together. The riverbank is a treacherous mudslide by the time we emerge, slipping and sliming our way from the primordial ooze. The cloud has emptied its load on us and the sun has come out the other side. The sun warms us, the ground steams in response and we loll on the damp grass, enjoying the post-exhilaration calm. Irrepressible smiles sent up to the sky...

Aboriginal Knowledge

The local inhabitants of an area will always know the most about their corner of the world and the Australian Aborigines are an excellent example of a people fully in tune with their surroundings. In the Northern Territories, where I was so ineptly interacting with the Australian bush, an understanding of water systems and how to find water was central to human survival. The Aboriginal people developed an intimate relationship with their land, based on their deep understanding, long before European settlers arrived; their need to understand water and the land shaped their culture. Travelling and hunting in an arid landscape is immensely challenging, as the European settlers found to their peril; it is only with their detailed knowledge of how to find the elusive elixir of life that the Aborigines could survive. In a culture without the written word, they devised stories and songs to pass on their beliefs and knowledge to future generations, who believed that their ancestors' songs had created the land. Knowledge was survival and therefore power, and individuals had to prove their worth before the elders would entrust them with it. The information from the creation stories is entwined in song and dance, and held within easily remembered stories and myths designed to provide all the necessary knowledge for finding food and water sources to safeguard future generations.

Swimming the Blues

Rain in our lives is seen as a metaphor for depression and the words of Longfellow were immortalized in Ella Fitzgerald's mournful hit song – but for wild swimmers the rain holds no fear. All it does is feed the wild waters and if we are already in the water then we are already wet – bring on the rain!

The blues are a natural part of life, which we all face to a greater or lesser extent, and we all have our ways of dealing with them. There is a significant body of evidence pointing to the emotional benefits of wild swimming – if the blues threaten to overwhelm you, it's time to head to the water.

NIGHT SWIMMING

The hours of darkness are rarely as dark as you imagine. Choose a calm, dry night with plenty of moonlight for the best and safest night-time swim. The frisson of danger that the dark imparts only adds to the excitement as you enjoy the extraordinary experience of even a familiar swim.

IT IS A MOONLIT, STAR-SPANGLED, HEAVY INDIAN NIGHT. The warm, sultry air wraps us in a thick blanket; there is no breeze to lighten the load, so we crawl to the river for some refreshment. The water is singing quietly as we approach, whispering its secrets to the overhanging tamarind trees as it bubbles around the rocks and flows slickly over steps into the

Skinny Dipping

I wanted the river. Its wildness. I wanted to strip

naked and let the water lick my skin.

FROM 'THE SECRET LIFE OF BEES'
SUE MONK KIDD, AMERICAN NOVELIST

Some waters just ask to be dipped in and an impromptu swim often requires a skinny dip. The exuberance of an impromptu swim is life-affirming and the sensation of water on the body is unbeatable. Just remember to be considerate of other water users and reserve this for quiet times. Consideration aside, swimming in your birthday suit is the ultimate in communing with wild waters – exhilarating and sensuous, the end game of immersion.

---

wide deep pool, and continues on its secret journey into the dense, tangled undergrowth downstream. Wading gratefully into the cool water, I feel like Alice stepping through the mirrored looking-glass, opaque and mercurial in the moonlight. After our swim, we perch in the shadows on submerged rock ledges, chin deep in the water. The sounds of the night are quite different from the daytime and the silvery light lends everything a dreamlike quality. As we sit, bats start to flit around the pool, diving at the water surface, so fast they are almost invisible, picking off insects one at a time. One almost

skims my nose but they never collide as they perform the most amazing aerial gymnastics on their night hunt. A slight leather flutter of the wings is all that I hear; I remember when I was younger I could sometimes hear bat calls – but not now.

Altered Perception

The night-time lends a wonderful quality to the water and brings a whole new frisson of excitement to wild swimming. The reduced visual input feeds our natural fear of the unknown. Moonlight and moon shadow lend their magical qualities, rendering a mundane view mystical and unfamiliar; disturbing shapes materialize out of mundane, everyday features, imparting a new dimension to the lights and colours of reflections and distorting our perceptions. Floating in the inky black water can be a vertiginous experience when you lose your sense of up and down.

With the limited visual stimulus, the ears become an ever more important source of information in the night. As we sit silently submerged I can hear scratching in the undergrowth, a rustling in the riverside grasses. Completely invisible at first, I become aware of a slight increase in density in the shadows beside the pool and then the exquisite head of a deer appears in the moonglow. Cautious, sniffing the air, I think it senses our presence but can't make us out. It lowers its head, nose dipping into the pool, setting off delicate ripples that spread over the water towards us. The deer looks across the

surface of the water and straight through me, deep dark pools reflecting the glint of the moon. She can't see me submerged in the shadows but she is alert and ready to respond to the slightest movement or sound. As she drinks in the dappled moon shadow, the stars start to come out, twinkling all around us like a diamond blanket. But something is not quite right; the stars are too uniform in size and spacing and are densest around the lower horizon of the surrounding bushes – how can be I seeing them through the bushes? It suddenly dawns on me – these are not stars, but fireflies. I am surrounded by an entire cityscape of dancing, flickering fireflies.

Embrace the Night

Once you overcome your fear of blind encounters, the night has all kinds of wonders to show you. Leave your flashlight behind and allow the undisputed ruler of the night – the moon, and its attendant stars – to take control, with more subtle distinctions of light and dark. Sounds and smells are more noticeable when our eyes are dimmed and a whole new array of plants and animals becomes significant. The coastal equivalent of the fireflies is the phosphorescence of marine plankton. On a clear, moonlit coastal night, you may be lucky enough to experience phosphorescence – when bioluminescent plankton congregate in the surface waters and emit light. Every stroke leaves a trail of shooting stars in your wake and your arms drip molten metal as you lift them out of the water.

SWIMMING SAFARI

◆

One of our most popular family entertainments is to take a swimming safari. With one person in the kayak, carrying water, food and towels, we all head off on a mini-adventure. We often take boogie boards and rubber rings for the younger members of the family, the older ones swimming freely.

Heading downstream, the joy of being in the river is evident in the noises we give off. It is great fun passing under bridges, listening for echoes, floating up to emerald-headed mallards and surprising walkers on the bank. An hour is just long enough for each stage before we stop for some refreshment and to regain our land legs.

Some planning is required to return to your starting point. Sometimes a curved river can mean a shorter walk back to the start. A circular route on a lake or there and back on a river or coast – if the flow and currents allow – are all great. If not, you may need to consider arranging transport at both ends of your swim – two cars, car and bus or bikes, taxis or trains.

A fun adventure is to follow a river right from its source down to the sea. For the great rivers of the world, this is a truly epic adventure of grand proportions. Martin Strel, the Slovenian 'Big River Man', has swum the entire length of several rivers. Most notably, he swam the Amazon, Danube, Mississippi and Yangtze, and holds many distance and time

world records. These kinds of adventures take months, if not years, of planning and require support teams, training and a considerable commitment from many people. The distances travelled are mind-boggling – the Amazon River is 6,400 km (3,977 miles) long. There are, however, considerably more manageable rivers that can be travelled in just a weekend.

Coastal Safaris

A coastal safari is a great way to enjoy the sea without the crowds – even in a busy area, you will easily find little-visited sections just off the beaten track. Just by swimming around a headland you can find yourself on your own deserted beach. Rocky coastlines are littered with caves, coves and inlets, bays with no path access, lagoons and grottoes with the most enchanting range of turquoise and aqua-green waters. Off-shore islands also often provide great opportunities for exploration. Each one is like an undiscovered Elysium land.

Like river safaris, coastal adventures require planning. You will need to check tides and currents to make sure that your planned swim is feasible and safe enough. The open water is less tricky but be cautious around caves, particularly those with narrow entrances; a small wave at the mouth of a cave or inlet can be funnelled into the small space, accelerating and increasing in height. It can be tricky at the wrong state of tide so if you are planning on going into caves, time it for the period around slack tide for maximum safety.

MINDFULNESS EXERCISE

AND... RELAX

※

Towards the end of your swim, take the time to warm down and stretch out all your hard-working muscles.

Concentrate on how your body is feeling, the strength in your muscles as your arms and legs move against the pressure of the water – if tensions develop in any of your muscles, try to breathe them away. On the next breath in, focus on the tight area and then as you breathe out hard, stretch out and feel the tension leaving that part of the body, dispersing into the surrounding water. Keep your neck long, as this is a common place to hold tension as you swim. As you make the inward stroke, feel the strength of your muscles as you tighten and pull yourself out of the water to breathe, then as your legs propel you forwards and you stretch out to reach for the next armful of water, blow all that tension and muscle contraction away with the outward stroke and outward breath. Any muscle tightness can be stretched out in this part of your stroke. I like to use swimming as a curative release for physical tensions as well as emotional tension. As you breathe out hard and stretch out your body, feel the physical and emotional tightness leave you and escape into the supportive water.

Notice how your breathing changes as you move from your power stroke to your stretched-out relaxed stroke, ebbing and flowing like the movement of the waves.

EXTREME SWIMMERS

There are some swimmers whose achievements I look upon with awe and wonder. Their swimming adventures are on the grandest scale, requiring huge commitments of time and energy – prolonged physical training is required, combined with extensive fundraising and logistical planning.

A SURPRISINGLY LARGE NUMBER of people have attempted channel crossings – from England to France, across the Bosphorus, from Honshu to Hokkaido in Japan, between North and South Islands in New Zealand. Possibly the most prestigious crossing, seen by many as the epitome of swimming challenges, is the English Channel (La Manche). Thirty-four kilometres (21 miles) between Dover in England and Calais in France, the Channel is cool water, with strong but manageable currents and a busy shipping channel. The rules and traditions that have developed around this crossing have strongly influenced the global open-water swimming community and are used as the standard for channel swimming challenges all over the world. One inspirational American lady, Lynne Cox, held the men's and women's speed record for crossing the Channel in 1972, at the age of fifteen. When it was broken, she reclaimed it the following year. Lynne went on to complete many extreme swimming challenges. In particular, she used her extreme swimming to unite countries. She swam

several channels in pursuit of peace between the countries on either side; most notable was her swim in the frigid waters of the Bering Strait. Forcing communication between the Russian and American nations in 1987, her swim helped to reunite communities on Big and Little Diomede Islands in the Bering Strait, who had been divided by the Iron Curtain.

Delight in the Sea

Lord Byron was famously the first official swimmer to swim the Hellespont, linking Europe with Asia. He suffered from walking problems but he was a proficient swimmer and proud of it. 'I delight in the sea,' he said, 'and come out with a buoyancy of spirits I never feel on any other occasion.' A more recent extreme swimmer, Sean Conway, decided to swim the length of Britain. This 1,448-km (900-mile) journey took four and a half months, with many physical and emotional challenges.

There are, however, many smaller open-water challenges that also provide a lot of fun and require much less onerous logistics. The popularity of these challenges is becoming so great that organized massed open-water swimming events are springing up all over the world. You could consider swimming around the Scilly Isles, across the Sea of Galilee in Israel, the Rottnest Island Swim crossing from Perth to Rottnest Island, numerous pier to pier swims, or round-island swims such as the annual Manhattan Island circumnavigation. If you find these challenges irresistible, the world is your watery oyster.

AUTUMN COLOURS

❖

And so we arrive at the next stage of our swimming story. The new challenge is to take on different water types, a variety of conditions, longer adventures or more challenging swims.

Using our newly developed skills, we now often find we are experiencing moments of flow – unconscious competence – where we swim in the moment without having to think and be aware. A moment of Zen and euphoria – a certain equilibrium.

We are now entering the autumn of our journey. It is time for us to reap the rewards of all the hard-earned growth and development, harvesting and enjoying the fruits of our labours. There is so much wild water out there; make the most of your experiences to get out and try some new adventures.

Autumn Highlights

Fire red ~ Burnt brown ~ Orange afternoon glow ~Warm water
Cold air ~ Jewelled spider webs ~ Leaves glow ~ Birds flock

Winds strip the trees ~ Nuts and berries ~ Squirrels squirrelling
Leaves carpet the ground ~ Burdock burrs ~ Mushrooms bloom

Subtle ivy flowers ~ Short evenings ~ Musty scents
Swimming through leaves ~ Night swimming

Harvest moon ~ Daddy-long-legs in the grass ~ Hips, haws
Nature's harvest ~ Damp rotting leaves

CHAPTER FIVE

REFLECTIONS FROM THE RIVERBANK

*Water is mesmerizing. We are drawn to the
water's edge and if we take time to sit and watch we
become absorbed. The infinitely changeable ripples and
reflections forming and reforming within their physical
constraints hold our attention, smoothing away mental
turmoil, until ultimately we find ourselves at rest.
As the reflections play on the water surface, take a
moment to reflect. Look deep into the water
and deep into your soul; allow yourself
to be inspired.*

CHANGING REFLECTIONS

◆

The world captured in reflection is imbued with interest and depth. The potential transience amplifies the magic of the moment. A gentle breeze or a landing insect ruffles the water, creating dancing lights and lines – shattering the image but creating unexpected beauty.

SITTING BY A LOWLAND RIVER reminiscent of the grey-green greasy Limpopo of Rudyard Kipling, I was drawn into its patterns. The day was still and the water as dense and impenetrable as a child's paintbrush water, but it still had a sheen like polished mahogany. Imposed on its murky background were surprisingly bright reflections of the lime-green bank opposite, the scudding white and grey clouds, the duck-egg blue sky. I could see the airborne world reflected beneath me; birds flew by and an aeroplane cut across the river, dividing it like a knife sharing a chocolate cake. The smooth river surface reflected everything so perfectly it was as if I were looking down into another world. But then some

◆

He thought his happiness was complete when,
as he meandered aimlessly along, suddenly he
stood by the edge of a full-fed river.

FROM 'THE WIND IN THE WILLOWS'
KENNETH GRAHAME 1859–1932, ENGLISH AUTHOR

◆

passing insects dropped by, landing on the water, setting up their concentric ripples and shattering the illusion. The clean cut of the aeroplane's contrail became the jagged edge of a toothed saw. The clouds shivered in their reflected glory. The tangential striations radiating from each insect scanned their way across the reflections.

Be Inspired

I could watch changing reflections in water all day long. Smooth planes of water flowing like rivers of glass over a lip of rock, the bubble and boil of churned-up water as it lands in a pool, the smooth surface of a lake, ripples playing across its surface, signposting the action of the wind, birds, fish and boats. The wide open ocean, waves and ripples, sunlight dancing and refracted. Like watching a roaring fire crackling in the hearth, the ever-changing constancy is at once soothing and completely absorbing.

Allow yourself to be healed and inspired

Not every day can be a swimming day, but the waterside environment is a great place for a moment of mindfulness – so even if your plans for a swim are frustrated, all is not lost. Don't miss out on the positive impact of water just because it is not the moment for a swim. Make the most of the water-side; sit back, kick off your shoes, breath deeply and take the time to look around; allow yourself to be healed and inspired.

EMOTIONAL BENEFITS

◆

Water in any setting enhances our efforts to find our Zen. As a water lover and water scientist practising mindfulness, I see that being around water, any water, has a huge impact on my mind and emotions — and I'm not alone in this. We are drawn irresistibly to the water — but why?

WALLACE J. NICHOLS has coined the term 'Blue Mind' — the invigorating peace that being in and around water inspires in us. There is lots of anecdotal evidence of the positive impacts of being around water but Nichols has brought together neuroscientists and water scientists to study and really understand the impacts and causes of Blue Mind.

As we have already seen, we need water, as we need oxygen, to sustain our lives. But more than this physiological need, we are inspired by water; our deep connection resonates through our history of art, literature and music, as well as our drive to interact with it physically — to sail, surf, swim, fish and create memories on its margins. Our interactions with water are intensely personal and individual. For some, it invokes positive emotions of excitement and deep calm; for others, it inspires more negative emotions of fear and trepidation. The premium we pay for waterside properties and hotel rooms with a sea view is universal. Is our physiological need for water so deeply ingrained that it drives our emotional responses to water?

Better All Round

The philosopher Dennis Dutton believed that we are hard-wired to love nature and gain psychological comfort from being immersed in it because 'mother' nature nurtures and sustains us. Studies carried out at Plymouth University, UK, in 2010 corroborate this phenomenon. Adults were shown pictures of urban and rural settings and asked to score them on how they impacted on their positive mood, preference and perceived naturalness. Rural settings scored higher than urban settings in general but interestingly all images that included water, whether in a rural or urban setting, scored more highly than the other images. Maybe this preference does come from our ancestral heritage, where our reliance on water lives on deep in our psyche.

Whatever the reason, it is clear that being around water makes the vast majority of people happy. And happiness should not be underrated. Happier people build better relationships, are more creative, more effective and productive at work. They cope better with problems, have greater self-control, are generally more charitable, show more empathy and cooperation. They have better immune and cardiovascular systems, resulting in greater longevity. They take better care of themselves and make better friends, colleagues and spouses. And not only is happiness positive for the individual and those around them, it also has a knock-on effect on those friends' friends and colleagues – it is a positive fan of influence.

If you ever needed an excuse to go out by the water, you have it now. As we begin to understand the human interaction with the water environment and the impact on our mental health, it has important implications for our wider world. Get out there and spread the love.

BRING YOUR ARTIST'S EYE

The importance of water in art is all around us and instinctively understood. Wherever there is water there is an abundance of artists, their creations inspired by the colours and light associated with the waterside as well as the emotional response that wells up as they absorb the setting.

WHEN YOU ARE BY THE WATER, take the chance to examine the details of the water and the wildlife. Take in the whole and then break it down – consider it with a photograph or a painting in mind. Look at the colour changes and the different shapes and textures of individual leaves on the plants, for example. How would you capture the curl of something as mundane as a nettle leaf – the interaction between light and shadow, the glint of light off the hairs? If this is a spot you visit regularly you may feel you have seen it all before, but look at the details – there is always more to see, and it changes with weather and light conditions. The pincushion detail of a plump patch of moss clinging to a

MINDFULNESS EXERCISE

TAKE A MOMENT TO REFLECT

✳

The waterside is the ideal setting for personal reflection, so start the exercise by getting comfortable. Find a place where you can sit and relax, settle yourself and have a few moments of breathing practice.

Once you are settled, focus on one particular stimulus for stress or anxiety in your life. Away from the everyday influences, it is possible to re-examine our personal experiences, thoughts and feelings without outside forces fogging our self-knowledge.

Start by considering your own role in the event, focus on your feelings. Try not to get swept along by extraneous thoughts that bubble to the surface and look at the issues non-judgementally – this is not an exercise in self-flagellation or apportioning blame, it is an exercise in understanding. Be kind to yourself.

Next, move on to the roles and feelings of others in this issue. Try to be as non-judgemental and kind to others as you were to yourself.

Use the new setting to reconsider the source of anxiety from a different perspective. Consider someone else's viewpoint. Think about how you may be able to deal with a situation differently to alleviate the stress another time. Try to keep yourself at the centre of the reflection – while we may be able to influence outcomes to some extent, ultimately we only have control over our own actions. Try to focus on the aspects over which you have some control and make your peace with those over which you have none.

The space and relaxed atmosphere of the waterside allows us to achieve a certain clarity around events and reach a level of understanding that was previously unattainable. Take a moment to consider how your mindfulness practice is impacting on your life and your interactions with others.

Find beauty; be still

FROM 'MOUNTAINEERING IN SCOTLAND AND UNDISCOVERED SCOTLAND'
WILLIAM H. MURRAY 1913–96,
SCOTTISH MOUNTAINEER AND WRITER

rock midstream or the crisping curl of a tangle of seaweed stranded at low tide. Don't be afraid to be immobile – allow yourself to sit and be drawn in; be amazed by it. Taking the time to look closely at the details of what is around us changes our relationship with the environment – never again will you pass by without noticing that patch of moss. Maybe you will spot the changing of the seasons and the turning of the world and surprise yourself by the experience.

Painting Water

The elusive, transient nature of water has frustrated artists for millennia and is one of the hardest elements of life to capture. Many different media have been employed – the Japanese woodcuts, relying on strong design in curls and swirls; the Chinese inks and silks, layers of colours blurring and blending to reflect the movement of the aquatic world. Watercolour would seem the obvious medium to capture the essence of wild waters. Just the water that you use to mix the paint can change the nature of the pigments. The mineral content, the amount of iron or salt and whether the water is hard or soft will all affect the way the pigments are displayed on your paper. The British artist J.M.W. Turner apparently used to submerge his canvasses in water after the first application of paint to help with the watery effect.

John Constable painted in the Stour Valley in Suffolk. He was strongly influenced by the sights and sounds of the river and the Flatford Mill workings. I have spent some time in this area myself – situated halfway between where my mother and I live, we use it as a central meeting point for walks along the river. I also worked on these rivers for several years, assessing river flows and investigating the animal and plant communities. In a letter dated 23 October 1821 to John Fisher, a collector of his art, Constable wrote: 'The sounds of the water escaping from mill-dams etc., willows, old rotten planks, slimy posts and brickwork, I love such things... As long as I do paint, I shall never cease to paint such places. They have always been my delight.'

Wherever there is water there is an abundance of artists

Water in Sculpture

William Pye is a contemporary sculptor in water who grew up swimming in the lakes of his parents' country house. Inspired by water, he has created some wonderfully fun and challenging sculptures of water spirals and waves. One of his most stunning pieces is the font in Salisbury Cathedral. Although this does not sound like the basis for an exciting sculpture, the font is truly breathtaking. The basic construction is a deep, cruciform bronze water trough with a waterspout at each corner. The trough is filled to the brim with water, which looks like a highly polished black marble surface and forms the perfect horizontal mirror to reflect every detail of the cathedral's stunning stained-glass windows, roof and arch construction. The water flows out at each of the corner spouts to create four glass-like arcs that disappear through a bronze grill on the floor. Absolutely sublime. If swimming in water can inspire this kind of mind-blowing creativity, it surely has to be worth trying.

Landscaping with Water

Lancelot 'Capability' Brown (1716–83) was a large-scale artist in landscapes. With hundreds of major commissions in England still worth visiting, he is recognized as inspiring generations of landscape gardeners. Brown understood the importance of water in our enjoyment of the landscape and always included it in his designs as a central element to his constructed views. He would shape vegetation, topography and water in order to achieve its capability – which also earned him his nickname. The water features he designed were often sinuous lakes, created to imitate a river winding its way through the landscape. Brown would lead the visitor past the water to invoke an emotional response.

SENSE SCAN

As you sit by the water, use your eyes; really look closely at your surroundings. Imagine you are about to paint a picture. Take in the colours and shapes and textures – the subtleties and nuances of the water and surrounding vegetation, ripples on the shoreline, the play of the light and the depth of shadows.

Close your eyes for a moment and take in the soundscape. Sounds around the water have their own beauty – the ebb and flow of waves on a gravel shore, the clanking of boat halliards and the cry of gulls and waterbirds all evoke a feeling of place. These sounds, when you focus on them, create an intimacy that may raise the hairs on your body when you hear them next.

Water has a particular smell. The salt and ozone scent of the ocean is very evocative to many. Rivers and lakes also have their own subtle smell – organic muds and slightly metallic waters. Many smells are stronger in humid conditions and the saturated air over water can lead to heady scents exuded by plants and animals.

Watery environments are a feast for the senses: the synthesized blue and yellow lights of indoors are replaced by the full colour spectrum of light; sounds and smells are subtle and natural, soothing and calming to body and mind – a gift in the pursuit of mindfulness. This moment, as we observe it, will never be quite the same again; come again to the same spot and the light will change and with it the sounds and the smells. Just by taking note and marking down this moment makes us alive to the preciousness of life. It brings our lives and nature together as one – it makes us complete.

THE MUSIC OF THE WATER

◆

There is a fundamental link between the sounds we hear and the emotions we feel. The reverse is also true – the way we feel affects the way we perceive sounds. This means that a positive feedback between our emotions and the music of the water escalates their impact on us.

EVERY STRETCH OF WATER in each season and every time of day has its own signature tune. Take a moment to sit by the water; close your eyes, breathe smoothly and allow the sounds to come to you. Feel yourself in the centre of your surroundings, your ears receptive, gathering in the sounds around you to be catalogued and noted. Focus in on specific sounds – the background of the moving waters, the gentle whispering of wind in the reeds, the shushing of sand as waves ebb and flow. See if you can pick out individual insects whirring or the song of different birds. Listen to the soundscape as if it were a piece of music – how do you think you would create the sounds into a musical score to capture all the elements into your own soundscape hit?

Watery Classics

Water has played a prominent role in the musical world. The sounds of the water are hugely evocative to us, making the hairs on the back of our neck stand up, and music can bring tears to our eyes. As a source of inspiration, water has been

the backdrop to a great many commissioned works of music, as well as the subject of a whole range of musical masterpieces. Classically and most famously, Handel was commissioned by King George I to create a piece of orchestral music for a party in 1717, which was to be performed on barges on the River Thames. The resulting three suites, Handel's 'Water Music', are instantly recognizable jaunty tunes, each suite being based on a different dance style.

A much wider body of music has been written that attempts to capture the imagery of water. 'Aquarium', a movement of Camille Saint-Saens' 'Carnival of the Animals', is very familiar, evoking beautifully the nature of the underwater ocean; it has been used extensively as a film and TV score. In Ravel's 'Jeux d'eau', the piano imitates the sound of playing water – bubbling in pools, trickling over stones, splashing over waterfalls and spinning in eddies. Ravel said it was 'inspired by the noise of water and by the musical sounds that make one hear the sprays of water, the cascades, and the brooks'. On the manuscript he wrote a quote from Henri de Régnier's poem *La Cité des eaux*, translated as 'River god laughing as the water tickled him'.

The water played like music around my head,
my shoulders shimmered in the sunlight.

FROM 'SWIMMING TO ANTARCTICA'
LYNNE COX, AMERICAN OPEN-WATER SWIMMER

The musical impression of a storm was popular in baroque music and the cresting waves and high drama of the seas are captured with great musicality and vigour by Verdi in his 'Tempest di Mare' – various pieces came under this name, one for flute and two violin concertos were part of his 'Four Seasons' work. Debussy has audibly reflected the nature of water in his piano pieces '*Reflets dans l'eau*' ('Reflections in the Water'). If you want to listen to some music to transport you to the riverbank, this could be the piece for you.

Active Listening

I am personally entranced by the work of Chris Watson, a contemporary musician and sound artist inspired by nature. Chris has captured the sounds of nature with his incredibly sensitive recording equipment and tells some amazing stories through his works. Have a listen to some of his recordings on YouTube. For example, in 'The Colour of Sound' he buries hydrophones (underwater sound equipment) on the shoreline so you can hear the sound a few centimetres under the surface of the sand. I challenge you to listen to the sounds without smiling – a deeply intense feeling right in the core of your being. In his narration, Watson suggests we have this feeling because the sounds are so close to our pre-natal experience; our sense of hearing develops well before we leave the womb and our embryonic hearing is therefore subaquatic. This could give some clue to our love of the sound of the sea. Chris has travelled all over the world recording sounds; he notes that 'no two oceans or seas sounds the same'.

Listening intently to the sounds around you will awaken your sense of hearing; sounds you never noticed before will reach into your mind with a musical quality. Listening actively is a creative activity that stimulates thought and allows you to think laterally. By awakening your listening mind and tuning in, you open up a whole new sonic world that is entirely absorbing and intensely stimulating.

WATER WORDSMITH

Every writer knows that the build-up to putting pen to paper is fun in its own right — conducting research and generating inspiration are invaluable to the writer's trade. And what better way could there possibly be to get in the mood for some sparkling wordsmithery than spending time at the water's edge?

WALKING TO SCHOOL YESTERDAY, my daughter and I went past the garage, where the owner was brushing down his forecourt with a stiff yard brush. We were deep in conversation but both stopped in our tracks as we recognized the unmistakable sound of the sea; who knew it? A good stiff yard brush sounds exactly like the hiss of the backwash over pebbles. I was instantly transported to a contemplative stroll along Holkham Beach in North Norfolk on a bright spring day.

The brook giggled as though it

had just seen some joke…

FROM 'PUCK OF POOK'S HILL'
RUDYARD KIPLING 1865–1936, ENGLISH POET AND NOVELIST

A Place of Infinite Possibility

Walking along the shallows of the beach, a horizontal banded theatre in the round, I turn on the spot and the colours and textures spiral up to the sky; strips of golden sands, white-striped breaking waves, lichen-green marram grass, silvery sea, British racing green Scots pines, dip-dyed blue sky and wispy strands of cloud stretching and extending up into the atmosphere.

The background noise of the sea sounds like the applause of an appreciative audience to the shrieking laughter of the gulls. The light is having a ball playing in the water; through the shallow water all around and over my feet, the slices of light dance and sway, refracted through the smooth wavelets; the choppy waves on the wider sea bounce the light around, catching vertices and edges, scoops and holes, sculpting light and dark; sudden shards squinting the eye.

Turning away from the sea, the shallow beach is so wide it almost reaches the horizon. I crunch over a band of razor shells, like so many grotesquely discarded false fingernails. Stride across a wide expanse of ankle-whipping sand; small pebbles form a constellation of comets, each with their own tail of wind-blown sand telling their tale of the prevailing wind. This is nature at its most expansive; there's nothing to interrupt your thoughts, no obstructions to imagination; just the sand, sea and sky as far as the eye can see. In this kind of setting, your heart sings and like Alice and the Red Queen you can imagine any number of impossible things before breakfast. A place of inspiration and infinite possibility.

Inspired Writers

Writers love the water. Ever since the beginnings of words, water has inspired writers and it has taken on many roles over the years. Wild water is used for its symbolism in many poems and stories but sometimes it is portrayed anthropomorphically, as in Ted Hughes' poem 'How the Water Began to Play' and the character of the Mississippi in Mark Twain's *Huckleberry Finn*. The Ancient Greek Homer and the Romans Ovid and Horace were all stimulated by water and inspired by its scarcity, while the Japanese were bowled over by its abundance; the expression of nature in their art made water an obvious subject for the haiku of Matsuo Basho. The sensuous nature of water was made much of by Gustave Flaubert, who wrote overlooking the Seine in Paris – caught up by the city's romance and watching the river as he worked, maybe this was inevitable.

The greatest of all minds, Leonard da Vinci was constantly exercised by water. He studied and observed it extensively, making copious drawings, carrying out experiments and writing many words on the subject. His handwritten Codex Leicester, the world's most valuable manuscript, is about one third water-related drawings, including the infamous sketch of the water droplet falling into water and displacing a crown-shaped splash. He illustrates beautifully in this work the link between art and science – the creativity that's required in the scientific process is a link we are in danger of losing in today's funnelled education system.

Inspired by Immersion in Water

Roger Deakins, in large part responsible for the renaissance of wild swimming in Britain, is perhaps one of the most well-known of recent wild water writers, spawning a whole series of wild swimming books in his wake. I only discovered his writing months before his death, which coincided with that of my own father, and I was inspired by the two men to write my first book for river lovers, *The River Book*.

Immersion in water has been used as a tool by many writers, from Lord Byron and Percy Bysshe Shelley to Iris Murdoch, Agatha Christie and Patrick Leigh Furmor, who returned daily to the water to soothe their furrowed brows and fuel their creative outpourings. If art and music are not your media, why not try to capture your observations and emotions in words? Try some alliteration and metaphors to describe the sights and sounds. Make the most of your proximity to the liquid elixir, take a notepad and pen and get down to work.

WINTER WONDERLAND

The year has come full cycle and the river has reached the sea. We have reached a quiet confidence in both our swimming and our mindful activities.

While we can be entranced by the vigour of spring, the blowsiness of summer and the mellow harvest of autumn, there is much pleasure to be gained in the hunkered-down cold of winter. Don't shut the doors in the winter months — get out and revel in its stark glories. There is much to enjoy in our winter wonderland in the water and on the shore and there is no better feeling than being wrapped up warm on the sofa when you have braved the elements.

Winter Highlights

Frozen sand ~ Deserted beaches ~ Heavy gelid waters
Snuggly jumpers ~ Easy access ~ No stinging nettles

Hot drinks ~ Hats and gloves ~ Gut-clenching cold
Skeleton trees ~ Honking geese ~ Magical wonderland

Quiet shorelines ~ Solitary swims ~ Silent sluggish waters
Hoar frosts ~ Pale blue skies ~ Frigid starry nights

Low sun ~ Long shadows, ~ Iron-grey water
Seering winds — cut like a knife ~ The buzz when it is done

CHAPTER SIX

WATER WISDOM

Water permeates all aspects of our lives
— ubiquitous but miraculous, often unnoticed and
frequently unappreciated, it drives all physical
processes and shapes our world. Now is the time to
notice, to pay attention and absorb some of the wisdom
of water. Use your wild swimming and mindfulness
experiences to feed into a richer life with greater
understanding and a broader view of the world;
spread the joy and swim towards new
territories without looking back.

THE AGE-OLD RIVER

◆

As with old age in man, the ancient river carries much with it. Every rock it has passed over and every industrial waste stream has left its mark. By the time the river reaches the sea, it has developed its own unique nature, reflecting its life experiences.

THE EXACT CHEMICAL NATURE OF THE WATER in a river acts as a fingerprint, identifying the river to the animals that live within it. A salmon is able to recognize the chemical signature of its parent river even when it is far out at sea, by following the traces of compounds right into the river mouth and all the way upstream to its spawning grounds. The vitality and uniqueness of each body of water is essential to the survival of the diversity of life. The same can be true of man. They say that in old age we get the face that we have lived. I hope mine will be creased with valleys of laughter, tough as old leather, tanned by days of open air and cold waters, my eyes pale with hours of looking to the sunrise.

A river in its old age is slow flowing, taking its time, dark with sediment – the rich wisdom that it is waiting to deposit for the fertility of the land as it spreads out on its way to the sea, feeding the soil and enriching the plant life in its water meadows and salt marshes. We must recognize the wealth of wisdom in our elders, not constraining them in the holding pens of nursing homes in the same way we divert and culvert our rivers and estuaries when they don't conform to our own convenience. Visit the last miles of a river and see the richness they divest in salt marshes, mangrove swamps and deltas the world over – vast areas of enriched vegetation, feeding shoals of breeding fish and flocks of wading birds.

Be Like the River Flowing

Water offers up much wisdom as it flows; consider the nature of the river and try to emulate it.

Healthy water is always moving. As you engage in the flow of life, make the most of opportunities, be open to influences and absorb information from all you encounter, and try not to stagnate. Use your mindfulness practice in moments of stillness to achieve clarity of thinking, to help you assimilate the good that you encounter into your life and discard what you know to be bad. As the river flows through sequences of calm pools, smooth, fast-moving water and turbulent sections, so you will encounter these phases of your life – still periods of quiet reflection, high-speed productive activity and chaotic, uncontrolled activity. They all have their place and their value – treat them as just part of the natural line and learn to go with the flow. Use the different phases to inform and nourish you as you continue on your journey through life.

Water offers up
much wisdom as it flows;

REAPING THE REWARDS

◆

There is much in the nature of water that we can emulate to good effect in our own lives. Flowing around obstacles or eroding them through persistent action, keeping fluid and mobile but choosing the moment to settle and find clarity, becoming indispensable — these are all characteristics we can employ.

THE JOURNEY IS ALMOST COMPLETE. We have practised and experienced much. We are mastering the art of mindful wild swimming, gradually becoming unconsciously competent. Ever more regularly we find ourselves in the flow, living fully in the moment and completely engaged in our wild swimming. Water can take 3,000 years to complete its cycle from falling to earth to regaining the atmosphere. Like the water circling the oceans, we will continue on through our life cycle; the seasonal cycles will go on and the world will keep turning. We will continue to master new skills, at first unaware of what we have to learn but eventually reaching mindfulness as we master unconscious competence.

Highs and Lows

Being in the water brings moments of great joy but also moments of great fear as we challenge ourselves both mentally and physically. When we swim we are exposed to the natural world, a world we cannot hope to control. As we learn to accept this fact, we can begin to let go of the outcome from a swim. This enables us to relax and enjoy the moment as it unfolds; we will regularly be surprised by the moments of great joy that we experience as we swim, those unexpected moments of light and clarity.

These heightened emotional highs and lows may be the reason we are drawn repeatedly to wild swimming – we will always try to emulate those occasions when time stands still, we are entirely focused in the moment, swimming smoothly without apparently having to try. They may seem as though they are a step outside of our everyday lives, something extraordinary, but the personal lessons we learn in the water are applicable as we move through our world. When we begin to understand and trust ourselves through the process of mindfulness in any setting, we have an immensely important skill that we can bring to life.

The personal confidence we develop in the water can be transferred to the challenges and obstacles we confront every

---◆---

Once in the water Iris cheers up a bit. It is almost too warm, hardly refreshing. But its old brown slow-flowing deliciousness remains, and we smile happily at each other as we paddle quietly to and fro.

FROM 'IRIS'
JOHN BAYLEY 1925–2015, ENGLISH NOVELIST AND LITERARY CRITIC

---◆---

day. Just knowing that we can breathe and move anxiety to the side for a moment allows us to deal with the ripples and whirlpools of life with greater equanimity, to find a route through the rough waters.

CATCH A FREE RIDE

Once you discover the joys of wild swimming, you will begin to see wild waters differently. A once familiar landscape develops a new dimension, offering the promise of exhilaration and excitement. Rivers, estuaries and seas are now opportunities for a free ride.

I T WAS A CLEAR WINTER'S DAY and although the roof had sparkled with the crystals of a light frost at dawn, the time had come to embark on a wild swim. I had long been thinking about catching the tide to ride up the estuary to the river. As ever, life intervened, but I still managed to reach the estuary to catch the end of the rising tide. The forecasters had been right – it had turned into a beautiful day. I parked the car and jogged on soft muddy trails the mile down to my start point. On a background of blue sky, billowy, swan-white clouds hung stationary. It was surprisingly sultry on the bank; the peaceful cooing of doves was, however, shattered by amorous magpies rocking the bare branches of the old oak.

The water perfectly matched the stillness of the winter's day. The surface, completely flat, appeared unruffled and dense

— the impenetrable brown of the hot chocolate in the flask I had planted on the bank at my planned exit point, anticipating the post-swim chill. The reflections of the boat hulls and their vertical masts, the solid blue sky and aerial white clouds were surprisingly bright on the opaque water. The black outline of the parkland oaks, still in their winter lack of foliage, was inked onto the margin between land and sky. Looking directly up, a distant aeroplane was only visible as a languorous shooting star, catching the sun on its way overhead.

The Swim

The sudden clatter and splash of a mallard taking off in fright and the aggressive craw of a crow disturbed in its tree betrays activity around me. The end of a waterlogged tree stump just emerging from the water's surface resembles an otter's head. I am distracted by it again and again, having to check several times before it finally imprints itself in my head as a tree stump and I stop reacting to its image in the corner of my eye.

My first toe in the brackish water reveals that it has nothing in common whatsoever with the warm sweet liquid waiting for me in my flask. My hands, once in the water, immediately ache as if holding ice cream straight from the freezer. The mirrored surface of the water, now at eye level, takes on the appearance of molten mercury. Silvery and reflective, bending and bulging in reaction to my displacement, undulating away, a watery downland stretching out towards the far bank.

Beginning to get used to the water, I stretch out upstream – whisked along at a brisk pace, I only swim to keep warm. Maybe the cold water begins to numb my senses but before long the ache in my hands subsides and the water feels quite pleasant on my skin. As I relax, my neck lengthens and my shoulders loosen. My strokes fall into a rhythm and my breathing calms too. I go with the flow for a while and then turn and power against the tide for a few minutes to fully experience the force of nature. I'm going nowhere and the bow-wave I throw up is making it hard to breathe, so I turn and enjoy my free ride, allowing the tide to carry me along. I plan to exit beside a bridge, which has a convenient shelving grassy bank and is an easy landmark. As I am carried towards it, I have to gather myself to swim to the side of the channel to exit the fast water. A few minutes of effort are required to angle my way across to my towel, clothes and warm flask.

Sitting on the bank after my swim, I feel elated and alive. The world seems suddenly brighter, more sharply defined; the sweet warmth of the hot chocolate warms me from the inside, my skin burns and glows from the action of the water, and my toes are still blissfully numb.

Hitching a Ride

As you develop your understanding of wild waters and build confidence in your wild swimming, you will learn to make the most of the attributes that different waters possess –

MINDFULNESS EXERCISE

GO WITH THE FLOW

✳

We rarely take time in our lives to just let things happen, to go with the flow. This exercise is all about letting go and allowing the water to support us and carry us along.

Start by ensuring that the waterbody you are in is safe to just float in, that you are not going to be carried away at speed. Once that is established, lie back and scull with your hands just to keep yourself afloat, but otherwise let yourself relax into the water. Watch the clouds, birds and planes passing overhead – like your thoughts, observe them passing by but try not to get too caught up in them.

Feel the water supporting you and think about where the water has come from and where it will be going – from sky to earth, underground, in rivers, lakes and seas, shallow bays and wide open ocean, caught up in man-made processes and industry, through bodies and plants, up in our atmosphere, caught tight in polar ice caps, flowing freely as water and floating up high as water vapour. Water travels to all areas of the world and our planet in its vast and never-ending cycle. Cycling and recycling.

Think about the journey you are on. Enjoy this moment where you are not rushing from one thing to another; you are not even dictating where you are going. See how it feels to be present in the moment, experiencing the movements of the water carrying you along. This moment of stillness is available to all of us, anytime, when we allow ourselves to go with the flow for a moment – just coasting. We can be frightened of what will happen if we just let time pass but it can be very liberating to let go for a short while, to see that our world does not collapse when we are not driving things.

swimming around the bend in meanders, hitching a ride with a river, and making the most of tides and currents in coastal waters. The nutrient-rich waters along the coastal zone can result in extensive areas of mud, which at first may seem unappealing. Further investigation of these zones – forming salt marshes in temperate zones and mangroves in tropical areas – reveals a rich wildlife community, some of the greatest diversity and abundance in the world. Estuaries can make very interesting swimming locations but require quite careful planning. Tidal influences combined with the freshwater flow down to the sea can sometimes result in complex currents that require local knowledge to unravel. Once understood, however, you can have a wonderful swim travelling with the incoming or outgoing tide to cover much more ground than would otherwise be possible.

FLOWING ROUND OBSTACLES

We may embark on a swim with high expectations and a clear idea of how we want the experience to be, but sometimes things don't go to plan. Not every swim or watery interaction will be perfect. Not everything is under our control.

THE WEATHER IS JUST ONE OBVIOUS FACTOR – other swimmers may drop out at the last minute, we may get cramp, not feel well or things may just not flow. Maybe you couldn't get your breathing quite right or you were constantly distracted by negative thoughts and you felt a failure in your attempts at mindfulness. Even the perfect day can be marred by the thought that it will soon be over and the next day may not have the same sheen.

Try to make peace with yourself about these feelings. They are an entirely normal part of the human condition. You don't have to like it but try not to let it get so big that it overwhelms you. When we are present in the moment, we are aware of what is happening; we can face the emotions and maybe even laugh at ourselves a little – diminish the negative thought and try to put it into some perspective.

Acceptance

So much of our dissatisfaction in life is born out of our desire for things to be a certain way. We all have an internal view of how things should go, an expectation of how things should be – a little checklist for life. When life does not follow our internal script, we can feel very dissatisfied. Hopefully, by approaching wild swimming mindfully we can prevent the frustration from overflowing. If you are fully engaged in your swim, you will be aware that your mind is being taken over by a fog of negative thoughts. Just acknowledging what is going wrong and witnessing your emotions makes it easier to relax into the moment, open your mind and move on to another reality, the one that is actually unfolding in front of you, with a sense of acceptance and possibly even enjoyment. Rather than holding on inflexibly and clinging on to certain outcomes that are subject to matters outside our control, we can be liberated and enjoy some serendipity.

Taken mindfully, obstacles can later reveal themselves as opportunities – when we go with the flow and make the most of life's amendments, great things can happen. As Mark Twain said, 'Name the greatest of all inventors. Accident.'

OUR WORLD

The world is ours to explore; it's where we come from and it is very important for our survival to remember that we are animals on a wild planet. If we allow ourselves to experience all the diverse beauty in the world and to challenge ourselves, we really come to life.

MUCH IMPORTANT WORK IS DONE behind desks and the reality of our modern world cannot be ignored; we will spend much of our working and studying lives indoors. However, if we can find a balance between sitting at a desk and getting out into the wild world, we will become rejuvenated; our strength and spirit will be invigorated. At the final count-down, as you sit rocking in your chair, you will not miss those extra hours spent sat at your desk – staring at the monitor, watching cute cat videos. The important things in life are the people you love and interact with, the places you visited and the adventures you had. We owe it to ourselves, our fellow inhabitants and our planet to get out and really live in our world.

Ripples of Influence

So wild swimming is great, we are living life to the full and enjoying the adventures. We are in the water – fully immersed and mindful, we have found our flow, we are smooth, tranquil and happy. We are feeling particularly pleased with ourselves. But what happens when we need to get back to the day job?

Back out of the water, we are instantly buzzed on our phone; the internet bombards us with images of success and beauty, making our own simple lives seem somehow lacking. Work and leisure commitments seem to take over any family time and we are constantly harassed, late and anxious. We can take steps to be more mindful – but if everyone else is still running around, where does it get us?

This is where we have to stand firm and remember what we have learned; as Ghandi said: 'Be the change you want to see.' We can only change ourselves and hope that the ripples will spread and influence those around us. If we can take a little of what we found in the water back to the boardroom, maybe that will rub off on someone else. Now is the time to see if our greater personal understanding can in fact help us with understanding others – whether we can communicate better and whether by being less judgemental of ourselves and others we can reach better outcomes.

So, when you find yourself getting lost in a spiral, take a moment to breathe, notice what is happening, and see if you can deflect it. And when it all gets too much, the river, lake, sea, open-air pool is always there. Consider taking someone with you and see if you can improve their day, too.

THE RESPONSIBILITY TO CARE

When we reconnect with wild waters, we learn how great they make us feel and how they benefit our lives in so many ways. The Earth is a precious organism and we have a duty of care to give our planet and ourselves the best chance of a healthy and happy future.

O N MY KITCHEN WALL I have the picture 'Earthrise', taken in 1968 on the Apollo 8 mission by Astronaut William Anders. The photograph is taken at the point where they saw the Earth emerging from behind the moon. The Earth really is a truly marvellous sight and as Arthur C. Clarke said: 'How inappropriate to call this planet Earth when it is quite clearly Ocean.'

Earth is stunning from space and it is pretty great on Earth too; however, by placing too great an emphasis on personal greed and growth economics, we risk losing everything because we don't take account of how important the world is to our survival. The Earth is a wonderful organism and nature is phenomenal at self-healing. Every time I see a building left untended or a road shut off from use, I marvel at the speed with which nature moves in and the diversity of life that springs up in a very short space of time. We need to rethink ourselves back into our position as part of the functioning planet. We are part of nature – we are not the crew on a space module. I believe that by taking responsibility for our actions and giving nature and the planet some space, it has some chance of healing itself.

How Wild Swimming Helps

Swimming in natural waters can help put us back in touch with our elemental selves. It reminds us that everything we do on this planet matters and that clean water should be accessible to everyone – and that it is not just for drinking and agriculture. We can all benefit from some of the health-giving properties of water to swim in, jump in, splash our friends with or sit beside and reflect on life. Once we feel the immense benefits we gain from being around natural waters, we will realize that they are worth fighting for.

◆

Everyone thinks of changing the world
but no one thinks of changing himself.

FROM 'THE SLAVERY OF OUR TIMES'
LEO TOLSTOY 1828–1920, RUSSIAN NOVELIST
TRANSLATED BY AYLMER MAUDE

◆

We can seem very small at some moments – nature is awe-inspiring, and we are only short-lived and transitory on this planet, a butterfly wing flap in the eternity of evolution – but we all have our part to play. We must not just live in the now but live *well* in the now – with an eye to the future. Like the butterfly's flap, there are ripples of influence from everything we do and we should carry the consequences of our actions with care. Now is the time to get out there, get in the water mindfully and see what a better version of you looks like. Spread the word and help more people to realize the love of water and to achieve the goal of being at one with our world.

Manifesto for Mindfulness

But for now I'm off for a swim. I shall walk; maybe I'll take my shoes off and go barefoot. I'll wade into the water, trying not to stop as I reach that difficult midriff point. The leaves are spreading out over the surface of the pool and the tree is in bud. I can hear the voices of the birds calling to one another, bouncing from tree to tree. My spirits are rising inexorably – the sun is burnishing the bracken on the crags above the pool and crystals spark in the rugged rocks. After losing myself in the water for a while, I'll pull myself from the elemental ooze, towel down, wrap up and delight in a flask of something warming. I'll revel in the post-swim glow – all smoothed out. This is my manifesto for mindfulness – seeking and maybe even finding Zen by the water.

Till I End My Song

There is nothing unusual in this love of water ...
I think it is the unbroken sequences of flowing water, the
unchanging destinies of streams, that seem to knit a man's soul with
the eternities. The rhythms of eddying pools, the rhymes of lapping
wavelets, bring peace through eye and ear, emphasizing by their
unceasing flow the unimportance of our passing lives. On and
on they glide, not merely for the brief moments of our attention
but through every hour of night or day, varying yet constant.
The dancing of a mountain stream may be as entrancing as
a ballet, but the quiet of an age-old river is like the slow
turning of pages in a well loved book.

FROM 'TILL I END MY SONG'
ROBERT GIBBINGS 1889–1958, IRISH WRITER AND ARTIST

Further Reading

Blue Mind, Wallace J. Nichols (Back Bay Books, 2014)

Caught by the River: A Collection of Words on Water, Jeff Barrett, Robin Turner and Andrew Walsh (Cassell, 2009)

The Cloudspotters Guide, Gavin Pretor-Pinney (Sceptre, 2006)

Haunts of the Black Masseur: The Swimmer as Hero, Charles Sprawson (Vintage, 1992).

'Happiness is greater in natural environments', George MacKerron and Susana Mourato (*Journal of Global Environmental Change,* 23(2013)992–1000).

John Constable's Correspondence VI: The Fishers (Boydell & Brewer Ltd, 1970)

The Living Mountain, Nan Shepherd (Canongate Canons, 2008)

Mindfulness: A practical guide to finding peace in a frantic world, Mark Williams and Dr Danny Penman (Piatkus, 2011)

Moments of Mindfulness, Thich Nhat Hanh (Parallax Press, 2013)

Ring of Bright Water, Gavin Maxwell (Longmans, 1960)

Swimming to Antarctica, Lynne Cox (Weidenfeld & Nicholson, 2004)

Three Men in a Boat, Jerome K Jerome (Penguin, 2004)

Waterlog, Roger Deakin (Vintage, London, 2000)

The Wild Places, Robert Macfarlane (Granta Books, 2007)

Wild Swim, Kate Rew (Guardian Books, 2008)

Websites

nt.gov.au/emergency/community-safety/crocodile-safety-be-crocwise (Crocodile Safety: Be Crocwise)

www.outdoorswimmingsociety.com

www.swimtrek.com

www.wildswimming.co.uk

www.wildswim.com (Wild Swimming Map GB and Northern Europe)

THE MINDFULNESS SERIES

The Art of Mindful Baking
Julia Ponsonby

*The Art of Mindful
Birdwatching*
Claire Thompson

*The Art of Mindful
Gardening*
Ark Redwood

The Art of Mindful Silence
Adam Ford

The Art of Mindful Singing
Jeremy Dion

The Art of Mindful Walking
Adam Ford

*Einstein & the Art of
Mindful Cycling*
Ben Irvine

*Galileo & the Art of
Ageing Mindfully*
Adam Ford

*Happiness and How
it Happens*
The Happy Buddha

*The Heart of Mindful
Relationships*
Maria Arpa

*Mindfulness and
Compassion*
The Happy Buddha

Mindfulness and Surfing
Sam Bleakley

*Mindfulness & the Art
of Drawing*
Wendy Ann Greenhalgh

*Mindfulness & the Art
of Managing Anger*
Mike Fisher

*Mindfulness & the Art
of Urban Living*
Adam Ford

*Mindfulness & the Journey
of Bereavement*
Peter Bridgewater

*Mindfulness & the
Natural World*
Claire Thompson

Mindfulness at Work
Maria Arpa

*Mindfulness for Black
Dogs & Blue Days*
Richard Gilpin

*Mindfulness for
Unravelling Anxiety*
Richard Gilpin

*The Mindfulness
in Knitting*
Rachael Matthews

*Mindful Thoughts
for Cyclists*
Nick Moore

*Mindful Thoughts
for Walkers*
Adam Ford

Moments of Mindfulness

Naturally Mindful

*Seeking Silence
in a Noisy World*
Adam Ford

*Zen & the Path of
Mindful Parenting*
Clea Danaan

INDEX

acceptance 133–4
adolescent phase 42–4
age 9–10, 64, 107, 124–5
Anders, William 136
Aristotle 64
art 109–13
Australian Aborigines 91
autumn 101

Basho, Matsuo 119
Bayley, John 127
Bering Strait 100
biological age 9–10
Blue Mind 106
bodies 68
brain 35
brain pruning 43–4
breaststroke 33, 48, 50, 52
breathing 29–30, 31, 35, 38, 98
    explosive breathing 36
    trickle breathing 36
Brown, H. Jackson, Jr. 83
Brown, Lancelot 'Capability' 112
Buddha, the 43
burn, the 85
Byron, Lord George Gordon 100

channel crossings 99
checklist 26–7
Clarke, Arthur C. 136
clothes 67–8
coastal waters 95, 97, 132
companions 69–76, 78
Constable, John 111
Conway, Sean 100
Cox, Lynne 25, 99–100, 115
crocodiles 88, 89
cycles 20–1, 39, 126, 131

Deakin, Roger 38, 120
Debussy, Claude 116
dry bag 27
Dutton, Dennis 107

earplugs 34
Earth, the 136
emotions 29, 37, 43, 66, 75, 92, 106–8,
    112, 127
estuaries 57–8, 132
extreme swimmers 99–100

Fisher, John 111
Fitzgerald, Ella 92
Flaubert, Gustave 119
floods 56–7
flying 79
front crawl 33, 36, 48, 50, 59, 87

gardens 112
Ghandi, Mahatma 135
Gibbings, Robert 139
Grahame, Kenneth 104

Handel, George Frideric 115
happiness 107
harbours 57–8
Heraclitus 12
hippocampus 35
Homer 119
Horace 119
Hughes, Ted 119

islands 97, 100

Kidd, Sue Monk 93
Kipling, Rudyard 104, 118

Lake Coniston 45–6
lakes 54–6
landmarks 48–9
landscaping 112
Langstrath Valley 74, 76
Leonardo da Vinci 119–20
longevity 107
Longfellow, Henry Wadsworth 92

McNish, Hollie 68
memories 75, 76, 78
mental health 10, 16
mindfulness 13–19, 28–30, 78
mobile phone 27
Murray, William H. 110
music 38, 114–17

neurogenesis 35
Nhat Hanh, Thich 31, 78
Nichols, Wallace J. 17, 106
night swimming 92–5
nose clips 34

open-air pools 60
otters 52
Ovid 119
oxytocin 66

painting 110–11
personal reflection 109
planning 26–7, 84
Proust, Marcel 20
Pye, William 111–12

quarries 56

rain 90, 92
Ransome, Arthur 45
Ravel, Maurice 115
reflections 104–5
Régnier, Henri de 115
relaxing 98
reservoirs 56
rhythm 9, 19, 31, 32, 35, 37, 38, 42, 85
rivers 56–8
route finding 48–9

safaris 96–7
safety 44, 72–3, 84
Saint-Saens, Camille 115
sculpture 111–12
seals 71, 72
seas 58–60
    coastal waters 95, 97, 132
    waves and swells 59
sense scan 113
silence 77
skin 66
skinny dipping 93
speeding-up 87
spring 39
stillness 125, 131
Stour Valley, Suffolk 111
Strel, Martin 96
summer 55, 61
Swallows and Amazons 45
swim skin 27

temperature 55, 65
tides 27, 132
Tolstoy, Leo 137
Turner, J.M.W. 111
Twain, Mark 119, 134

unconscious competence 20, 83, 101, 126

Verdi, Giuseppe 116

water 64–7, 124
waterfalls 86–9
waterside 105, 106, 109
Watson, Chris 116–17
weightlessness 79
wetsuit 27
White, T.H. 79
white water 57
wildlife 51, 52, 71, 72, 88, 89, 94–5
Williamson, Henry 52
winter 55, 121
writing 119–20

ACKNOWLEDGEMENTS

Who would have thought that from my first leap and splash into
water as a toddler that a whole lifestyle could be born. My greatest thanks
must go to my parents, Jill and John Turner, and my earliest swimming teacher,
Jane Asher, who have inspired and influenced my career and my life choices.

My sincere gratitude goes to the beautiful people of Leaping Hare Press;
firstly Monica Perdoni who remembered me from a meeting years ago and drew
me in to this project but also my special thanks go to Caroline Earle, Jenni Davis,
Graham Robson and Michael Whitehead for all their energies on behalf of the book.

My never-ending love and appreciation goes to my friends, family
and Alfie, who have all braved the wild waters with me; this is in memory
of all the adventures, sharp intakes of breath and happy times.